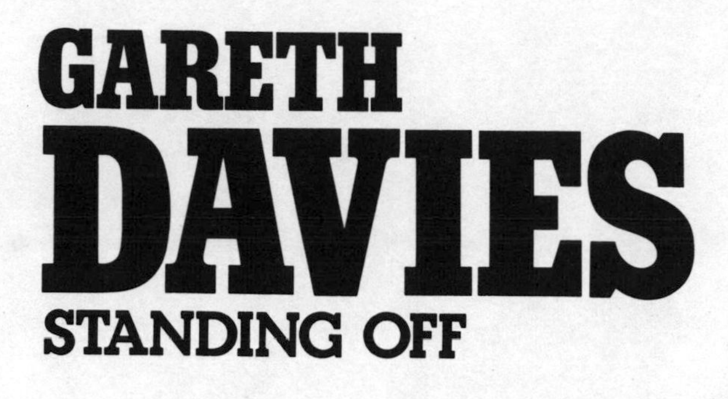
GARETH
DAVIES
STANDING OFF

GARETH DAVIES
STANDING OFF

MY LIFE IN RUGBY

Gareth Davies with Terry Godwin

Macdonald
Queen Anne Press

A Queen Anne Press BOOK

First published in 1986 by
Queen Anne Press, a division of
Macdonald & Co (Publishers) Ltd,
Maxwell House, 74 Worship Street,
London EC2A 2EN

British Library Cataloguing in Publication Data

Davies, Gareth
Standing Off: My Life in Rugby.
1. Davies, Gareth 2. Rugby football players
—— Wales —— Biography
I. Title II. Godwin, Terry
796.33'3'0924 GV944.9.D3/

ISBN 0-356-12157-7

Photoset by Cylinder Typesetting Limited, London
Reproduced, printed and bound in Great Britain by
Hazell Watson & Viney Limited,
Member of the BPCC Group,
Aylesbury, Bucks

ACKNOWLEDGEMENTS

I am indebted to my father, Elvet Davies, of Tumble, Paul Rees of the *Western Mail*, and John Jenkins, from Bow Street, Aberystwyth, for their help with this book. They drew my attention to items of which I had little or no knowledge, confirmed and unearthed facts and figures, and generally gave substance to some of my more hazy memories.

GARETH DAVIES,
Cardiff
August 1985

To my wife, Helen, for her love,
friendship and understanding

CONTENTS

	Preface	9
1	Why I Quit	14
2	Playing the Game	22
3	Tumble	32
4	Gwendraeth	45
5	Cardiff	56
6	From UWIST to Oxford	69
7	Portrait of a Partnership	81
8	Englishmen Abroad	91
9	1956 and All That	104
10	Inside Number Ten	113
11	The Day of the Coach	124
12	The Barbarians	135
13	A Traveller's Tale	142
14	The Future	154
	Career Statistics	168
	Index	173

PREFACE

When I first decided to put my career memories into print in this book, some close friends invested me with well-intentioned advice – and what are friends for but to advise and counsel in important decisions? Their suggestions were far-ranging but fell into two general categories. The first was that I should without qualification tell the truth, the second that I should be heedful of causing insult or displeasure. Respect and admiration would follow if I obeyed the first piece of advice, I was told, but I could finish some way down the popularity polls if I ignored the second. That these respective warnings seem to conflict with the old adage that the truth sometimes offends at first presented me with a bit of a dilemma, until I realised that very few things have marred a thoroughly pleasurable sporting life. Even though occasionally I crossed swords with one or two characters there was never cause for rancour or bitterness, either at the time or since. My story, therefore, I hope will present itself as it was: a marvellous experience, mostly of fun and pleasure. I am grateful that I was lucky enough to have had the chances that others have not. What disappointments there were were momentary, even illusory.

Naturally, in a game which arouses as much passion as rugby does, you do not always see eye to eye with everyone. In this regard, I hope the reader will find my experiences and comments illuminating and interesting. I think it behoves me to relate my views on certain aspects of the game, which I believe to be in the public interest. The strong opinions I nurture largely concern the future of rugby football in Britain generally and in Wales in particular. I believe my chief debt to the game which has given me so much pleasure should be repaid by drawing attention to the issues that I believe are important, or are in danger of being overlooked as the sport becomes a major leisure activity worldwide. I hope too that the fact that I am a fan of a great game becomes self-evident. I wish it nothing but success.

My enjoyment started at the beginning, at Tumble County Primary School, and continued with only a few hiccups through Gwendraeth Grammar School, Mynydd Mawr Schools, Tumble RFC, Carmarthen County, Welsh Secondary Schools, Llanelli, UWIST, Oxford University, Cardiff, Barbarians, Wales and the British Lions. I have worn other jerseys in that kaleidoscope of a career but all had one thing in common: they meant meeting interesting and kind people and forging friendships that have lasted and that sustained me when things did not go quite according to the script. I can contemplate few better occupations than travelling the world, as I've done, in the company of friends. There is no way I would exchange my experiences or my sporting career for anything (though I should admit that life *might* have taken a few different turnings had I been introduced earlier to the joys of golf).

My long involvement with Cardiff understandably represents a major slice of the action. The pleasure of playing with them, particularly during the past four years, has been immense. We have been very lucky to have stayed as a team for five or six years, and some strong bonds of friendship will continue long after the boots are finally thrown into the dustbin. Cardiff is not only about players; and I have many reasons to thank the committee and the Arms Park ground staff, notably Albert Francis and Bill Hardiman. As a non-'Kardiff' boy, I was not accepted by the supporters in the early days, but thankfully they've overcome their prejudice, it seems. After 11 years I feel like a part of the furniture there, if a little frayed at the edges like my blue and black hooped pyjamas. Playing for Cardiff has been an invigorating experience, and I shall never forget the reception the crowd gave me at the Arms Park a couple of days after I announced my retirement from international rugby.

Few sportsmen go through their careers without the support of a woman, and Helen, the woman in my life from the time we were at school together, has shown massive calm and intuitive understanding. I'm at present trying to re-educate her in the demands of my new front line activity, golf, but strangely her generosity and tolerance does not extend quite as far as it has done with rugby. That's the trouble with Welsh women – they think rugby is everything in a man's life when we all know, don't we, that it's not.

If I've been lucky at home and with my leisure, I have also been fortunate in my employment. It is not beyond the realms of possibility that I could by now have been an out-of-work miner, so I am especially grateful for the judgement shown by my employers in giving me my job in the first place and their patience since. I started with the Burnley Building Society in 1980 and have continued with the National & Provincial after their merger. I've sometimes groused at, but always respected, the house rule that if I wanted to tour, I had to use my leave. I'm particularly grateful for the counsel and friendship of Bob Stanley, my regional manager ever since I started. No-one could have had a better office staff, either. Sue and Tina, Margaret, Sheila and Gwynfor should all have been in the diplomatic service.

It now seems a very long time since it all started, of course, back in Tumble. Mam and Dad, bless 'em, may have had other expectations, but I hope they aren't too dissatisfied with the way things have turned out. They brought me up properly, with Victorian ideals, and they gave much to allow me my chance. This lastly, but not the least, is something for which I shall always be grateful.

'There is no chapel on the day on which they hang a man'

Oscar Wilde

1
WHY I QUIT

The charade came to an end on the afternoon of 12 April 1985. That was the day I rang the Welsh Rugby Union and told Malcolm Lewis that I no longer wanted to be considered for international selection. I'm glad it was Malcolm I spoke to, rather than anyone else. I'd always been friendly with him, and I had respected his contribution as assistant to John Dawes, the National Coaching Organiser, and he and 'Syd' had always struck me as genuine, people who understood players and their problems better than many others in the WRU. I think Malcolm was mildly shocked at my decision. He had always supported me in my three years out of the Welsh team and was ever optimistic of my return one day. Now, after he had seen me regain my place earlier in the season, as he had forecast, here I was telling him that I no longer wanted to be part of the Welsh set-up. He tried to get me to change my mind: 'Hang on now. Think about it. It's a very, very big decision you're making'. I was grateful for our chat and Malcolm's attempt to dissuade me. But the point was, I *had* thought about it, and nothing he or anyone else could say was likely to change my mind. I'd made the decision, as it happened, much earlier. I had informed the WRU merely out of courtesy.

It was not a decision made easily or in panic or rage. I'd had time to think long and hard, and I'd talked the matter over with my wife and also with Terry Holmes. If I needed influence, and counsel, it came from them.

It had been a strange week, really. There had been much speculation as to what sort of side Wales would pick to play

England (the match having been postponed from earlier in the season) and although I was the man in possession of the No. 10 spot, as it were, I had few illusions. I was quite prepared for the possibility that I might lose my place for this final match of the Championship. I had plenty of reason to think that Malcolm Dacey was still John Bevan's blue-eyed boy and that even if he was only 75 per cent fit he'd be voted back in. Had they dropped me and picked him in a straightforward manner, I would not have held up my arms and protested 'unfair'. Nor would I have entertained any great feeling of rejection. I would have been disappointed, of course, but not bitter. Even if Dacey had come back by means of orthodox selection there might not have been any reason to relinquish my ambition to continue playing for my country. As events turned out, I felt that I was left with little choice. Even in retrospect I think I was right. It was almost as if the action the selectors took – the naming of A.N. Other at fly-half – was calculated to force a decision from me, a provocation to which they knew I was bound to react.

I discovered their intention quite accidentally, before their freakish decision, and the team, was made public. I had gone to watch Cardiff play South Wales Police on the Wednesday night. During the match, one of the Cardiff alickadoos came up to me: 'Is it true?' he asked, 'They've picked A.N. Other?' It was obvious that the information had leaked out earlier that evening, and once again a player – in this case me – was being placed in a ludicrous position by the Big Five's seemingly chilling indifference towards the effect such a decision could have on a player. A.N. Other could imply only one thing – the selectors had no faith in the man in possession of the No. 10 jersey. Even if it was not a cynical device to express that view, it was at best ham-fisted.

The team, plus our friend A.N. Other, would be named the next day, Thursday, and I realised instantly how absurd, how invidious my position would appear to everyone. My heart sank. I felt desperately low, friendless, someone to be ridiculed and abused. It seemed unfair and unwarranted. If Dacey had got the nod in a straight fight or a vote, then so be it. But for

A.N. Other to hold the position until the selectors had another look at us – and other candidates – at forthcoming weekend club matches was bizarre. The message, however, was loud and clear. My suspicions that I was not really wanted in the team, and had not been wanted all season come to that, seemed confirmed. I went home like a man condemned. Helen, my wife, is the most unemotional, unflappable person you could meet. Even she mirrored my disappointment. She was tamping, as we say in Wales when someone is a trifle upset, over what we agreed was the final indignity. We talked about it until the early hours, agreeing eventually that I should bow out. The next day the team was announced. The phone fairly hummed with incredulous callers, mostly from the Press. I rang Holmesy. I told him I was going to quit. As captain of Wales he was, understandably, fairly non-committal, but as a friend he was sympathetic. He left me in no doubt as to what he'd have done if he had been similarly treated. I knew then that I was about to make the right decision. Well, at least it seemed the logical step. I resisted telling the Press. The WRU should be the first to know, I decided, because in the circumstances that was the right and proper course of action.

Eventually I spoke to Rod Morgan, the chairman of the selectors. In fairness to him, he tried to make me reconsider, asking me to wait until Saturday night at least, by which time the selectors would have seen myself, Dacey and young Jonathan Davies in action. I told him that the A.N. Other 'selection' made that impossible, that my confidence was totally undermined. 'It's perhaps not what it seems', Rod said. I replied: 'Even if I wait until Saturday and even if I am then picked, I honestly don't feel that I'd be in the right frame of mind to play, to produce the goods'. Finally, Rod asked me to hang on at least until the next day, Friday. If I hadn't contacted him by mid-day then, he said, he'd know that my decision was final. I didn't ring him. My career with Wales was over. The relief was profound.

It is interesting how my retirement was received. I had literally hundreds of letters from all over the world, and none of them castigated me for the way I dealt with it. David Hands, writing in *The Times,* declared that I had withdrawn from contention 'with dignity'. By contrast a selector, replying to a question about why I had not been told that I had not been picked, said: 'Why should he be told – just because he's got 21 caps?' How puerile that remark was. Surely, all one asks for is common courtesy, to be informed of a decision which, in a rugby-mad country like Wales, is bound to be of enormous personal importance. What on earth leads them to believe we players have no feelings, no emotions?

After seven years connected with the Welsh team, and 21 caps, it might seem faintly absurd, even illogical, that I hadn't come to terms with the vagaries of selection. After all, I had been dropped twice before (in 1981 and 1982), and the first time I came back it was to captain Wales; the second I returned after three years in the wilderness. Surely those experiences should have been potent lessons in the weird and whimsical world of national XV selection. Nothing should have surprised me.

I often reflect on my naïveté in the early days. I wanted to play for Wales so badly that it hurt. The anxiety, the anticipation, those sleepless nights that were followed by marvellous, heady days after I'd won a place in the team seem a long way away now. Quite a comparison, indeed, with the devastation I felt over the A.N. Other incident, which was in its way more hurtful than being dropped three seasons earlier, or even in 1981, when I felt I had been treated a little unfairly. In 1981 Wales lost to Scotland because our forwards were beaten, but it was the backs, J.P.R. Williams and Steve Fenwick included, who were made the scapegoats. Then, in 1982, after the débâcle against Scotland at the Arms Park, the axe came out again. I was luckier than the alleged conspirators in that defeat. Ray Gravell, Alun Donovan, Gerald Williams, Alan Phillips, Clive Burgess and Rhodri Lewis never played for Wales again.

There are, of course, aspects to being dropped other than personal feelings: the hurt and even the embarrassment. I wonder how the selectors would contend with walking down the street, being hissed and sneered at and being subjected to torrid verbal abuse. This happened to me, and I felt so humiliated by it that I very nearly decided to quit the game altogether. The world seems a cruel and unfriendly place to a fallen sports star. You have to put on a brave face, of course, and having dismissed the idea of dark glasses and blond wig, generally I found the best policy was to ignore the abuse of the street. I surprised myself how well I coped. On one occasion, however, I did crack. During a Welsh Cup semi-final against Newbridge at Newport, a provocative element in the crowd really got to me, and I prickled with rage. Alan Phillips, well versed in crowd behaviour, realised at once that I needed his advice. We had been awarded a penalty near the halfway line and Alan strode towards me. 'Kick the goal, that'll shut the bastards up.' The kick was a long one, for me, but I obliged. Alan was certainly right. It quietened the loudmouths, to my relief. Later in the clubhouse, however, it was obvious that one of them was still deriving some odd pleasure from keeping up the jibes. The club was crowded and noisy but even so the insults flowed loudly. For the first time in my life, red mist clouded my eyes and annoyance became rage. Something certainly snapped. Although Mr Bigmouth had his back to me I lashed out with all the power and strength I could muster from my 11½-stone frame. We shall never know whether it was a good punch or not – it missed by the proverbial mile. Suddenly all the Cardiff players who had witnessed my pugilistic foray burst into laughter. The punch had made Bigmouth turn round. He stood there open-mouthed. But it was his right arm, plastered and in a sling, which had caused the hilarity. 'You big bully,' they chided, 'fancy having a go at a cripple.' I didn't know whether to laugh or cry.

I suppose I am fortunate that people seem to have short memories. As my three years out of the big rugby scene drifted by – I was not even rated by the selectors in the first four fly-halves in Wales for most of that time – no-one seemed to care very much that I had been dropped, or whether there was any justification for it. I was the has-been, the forgotten man, and as John Bevan succeeded John Lloyd and John Dawes as coach, and promised a brave new world for Welsh rugby, I may have been fortunate that I was not part of that unfulfilled dream. I might have been blamed again. As it was, I kept plugging away for Cardiff, playing I believe the best rugby of my life. Certainly I was a better all-round player during those three years of exile than I was when I was first played. I recognised I had little chance of ever getting back into the Welsh side, but all the time I hoped that maybe one day I'd get the chance. Even after all the disappointments, I still wanted to play for Wales. I wanted above all else to prove the selectors wrong. The tremendous support I got from the players at Cardiff during this time sustained me – and I'll never forget it.

When Malcolm Dacey was injured and there was no other obvious candidate to call upon, I suddenly found myself invited back to the Welsh squad. I don't believe I was really wanted, or that I was a popular choice with the selectors. Indeed I had plenty of reasons for believing that neither Bevan nor Terry Cobner believed I could fit into their idea of an 'expansive' game, whatever that might mean. Well, I did make it, but only, I learned, by a 3-2 vote, and that at a time when the first choice Dacey was out of the reckoning completely. Obviously I was thrilled that I had returned. But what I had not taken into account was the reaction, my attitude. It was extraordinary, but I didn't really feel part of the Welsh team. Of the three internationals I played in in 1985, I didn't enjoy one. The selectors' obvious lack of confidence in me, the fact that I was really only the understudy, left me in no-man's-land. I'll never know, I suppose, whether I played the game they wanted me to play, but what I do know is that the type of game we did play was foreign to me. It was certainly different in many respects to the style which Cardiff, for example, had successfully employed for the past four years. In retrospect perhaps I should have rejected the Bevan Plan of trying to run the ball from all points and instead should have played my own natural game. The fact that I wasn't in control, calling the shots as fly-halves ought to, that I was not required to be the general in midfield – a role allocated to Bob Ackerman – plus that lack of confidence had a withering effect. I don't believe I played badly. But then again I did not play well.

Part of the problem can be traced back to squad sessions. They were tedious, and unproductive, and the atmosphere always seemed tense and uneasy. It was a complete contrast to my days with Dawes and John Lloyd. I suppose it didn't help my cause that I looked for contrasts. Previous squad sessions may have been too relaxed with no urgency on anyone's part. Now, however, they had gone to the other extreme. The Welsh squad system under Bevan in 1985 was a dictatorship, and apart from the fact that none of the players seemed to enjoy the sessions, the most debilitating element was that the system dampened individual flair and thinking. It was a bit like the old Army saying: 'you're not paid to think, but to do as you're told'.

Now none of this would have been important, and perhaps it would have been grudgingly accepted, if Wales had been winning and winning in style. But they were not. We may have meandered in previous years – under Bevan we completely lost our way in a jungle of conformity, team-work and set moves. That's the price you pay for taking the game out of the players' control and handing it over lock, stock and barrel to a coaching system. Perhaps as one of the senior players in the squad I should have spoken out, offered a contribution, tried to break the mould. I didn't and I'm sorry, though I don't think for a moment it would have made any difference.

I believe that if a squad system is to work properly it should be geared to getting the best out of each player. Confidence and encouragement of the individual should count more than set moves repeated *ad infinitum.* A bored player is a bad player and a bad player will play badly. Coaching has a lot to answer for.

When I did call it a day, it was a relief, as I've said. The lack of enjoyment latterly with Wales, thank goodness, has not left me embittered. The good times were many more than the bad, and even if some people seemed to go out of their way to sully the later years, they did not succeed. I've had a lot of fun, and but few regrets, and I've laughed more than I've cried.

'There is plenty of time to win this game'

Sir Francis Drake

2
PLAYING THE GAME

Apart from my last few internationals, whenever I played for Wales it was like winning my first cap over and over again. Nothing else I have done in rugby has equalled the anticipation, the thrill and sense of achievement of representing my country. All sportsmen have peaks of ambition, but I suspect few ever match those incredible, unforgettable moments that a Welshman experiences as he runs out at the Arms Park. You are tense, edgy and wet-palmed as you file out of the changing-room, but as you run down the tunnel, and then out into the cauldron, your heart thumps wildly beneath the red jersey, your legs turn to jelly and you gasp breathlessly as you are engulfed by the numbing noise, the myriad colours and the swirling, surging expectancy all around. Those first few seconds, when your brain struggles momentarily to cope with it all, stay with you for life, a sort of time capsule of emotion. Give or take a few missed heartbeats, it has always been like that for me, and if the subsequent 80 minutes have been on occasions rather more forgettable, the special initial thrill was always there.

I'm certain I'm not alone in having enjoyed that experience. I have yet to meet a player who has not been affected similarly. The reason I introduce it at this point in my nostalgia is because I believe there is a need to scotch the cynical speculation that seems to abound that playing for Wales is not what it used to be, that players have become apathetic, even blasé, and that the honour has somehow been debased because in recent years we have not fulfilled our own high standards in the international arena.

Ah, I can hear the cynics say, are you not overlooking the number of Welsh players who have recently declared their premature retirement from international rugby? To a man, did they not all say they were quitting because they no longer enjoyed it?

My response to that is simple. If the Welsh selectors were to invite, say, Graham Price, Spikey Watkins, Eddie Butler, Dai Richards, Jeff Squire, myself or any other recent defector to play again, even for a one-off match, I'm convinced every one of us would leap at the chance. Unless I have got my information wrong, or my understanding of the situation is warped, those that have quit did not do so because they did not want to play for Wales, but because basically the *preparation* for playing, the squad system etc., was not enjoyable and in their view that preparation was misguided, and was undermining the whole effort of producing a successful Welsh side.

It is important, I think, to stress the difference between the two. I am optimistic that at least one selector, the newly-installed Derek Quinnell, seems to have recognised the point the defectors wanted to establish, and has set store by his belief that the first priority is to get Wales back on the winning path. The style in which that should be achieved is significantly less important. While I acknowledge that this view will not be universally endorsed, I'm sure the thinking, should it prevail, will open up an entirely new attitude and introduce a refreshingly different sense of purpose within the Welsh set-up. If the drop-outs have helped bring about a change of direction, then the 'sacrifice' has been worth it. We all dearly want Wales to succeed, whether we are part of the team or not.

I'm lucky, I suppose, that I survived my international career without experiencing any sense of bitterness. Even though my last few matches weren't exactly pinnacles of personal performance, I can look back over my 21 matches for Wales with a feeling of satisfaction. It would have been even better had we won every time, but that smacks of Utopian values, and in the real world you have to accept the rough with the smooth. Wales have had some glorious periods, those so-called golden ages, and even if my period in the Welsh jersey did not match the glitter and the glory, it wasn't really all that bad in comparison.

It is extraordinary how often Australia have featured in my rugby life. I gained my first schoolboy cap against Australia, my first senior caps against them (in 1978), and my first match as captain of Wales was against them (1981). I have also played twice for Cardiff against the 1975 and 1984 Australians, and for the Barbarians in 1984. If one thing distinguishes the Aussies from all other sides I have played against it is their capacity for improvisation. Not one of the sides I played against could be called a great one, but each of them was tenacious and difficult to beat. Their athleticism, particularly among the forwards, seemed to give them an edge, and the only way you could blunt that effectively was in a tactical or footballing sense.

When I returned from the 1978 tour of Australia, jubilant that I'd become a Welsh player, I was presented with an entirely different experience – playing against New Zealand at the Arms Park. If I had to name my biggest disappointment in defeat it would be this match, because we were a better side on the day and we had victory snatched away only because of a referee's brainstorm. John Dawes, at his inspirational best, had built up the confidence in the Welsh team to such heights that we were absolutely convinced we would win. We were all going to be legends in our own lifetime, remembered and lionised for years. Victory was ours, too, eagerly grasped, only for the dreams to dissolve with Brian McKechnie's late penalty goal, that gift of cruel fate and errant refereeing. That day was a miniature eternity, and I kick the cat whenever I think of it.

It is often overlooked that out of that defeat there emerged a new purpose in Welsh rugby, and by the end of the season (1978-79), we had consolation aplenty because we beat Scotland, Ireland and England to win the Championship and the Triple Crown. The Scotland match, at windy Murrayfield, was for Terry Holmes and myself a perfect beginning to our partnership in the Championship, and although the Irish gave Wales a searching test, by the time we beat England by the biggest margin for 74 years (27-3), we confidently felt we were part of a very good Welsh side, if not a great one. The fledglings had emerged from their home public examination and the critics dubbed us suitable successors to Gareth Edwards and Phil Bennett. It was new faces all round, of course, for 1979 was the year when many great players bowed out from the international scene, including Mike Gibson, Ian McGeechan, Peter Squires, J.J. Williams, Ian McLauchlan, Gerard Cholley and Derek Quinnell.

Although Wales won only two Championship matches in 1980, I always regard that season as my best internationally. We got off to a good start, beating Romania, although it was not until much later that someone pointed out that my two dropped goals in that match constituted a rare feat in international rugby. I reckon I had my most satisfactory match ever, in all-round terms, on 19 January in Wales' convincing 18-3 win over France at Cardiff. Confidence is everything to a fly-half, and with our pack sending back a stream of good possession, I felt compelled to give everything a try. I was marked by Caussade, but I never saw him, nor very much of Rives. I looked for spaces and found them, and ran the ball more often than I've done in any international. Terry Holmes described my kicking as shrewd and I suppose I enjoyed turning the screw on the French. Dai Richards, Graham Price, Terry and Elgan Rees scored the tries, and honestly, we should have blitzed them. Elgan's eager but butter-fingered snatches lost him a golden chance of breaking the Welsh try-scoring record.

Our next match, at Twickenham, was the notorious 'Paul Ringer' match. It was very physical, often nasty, but when the Welsh pack was down to seven, I realised I had to play the best game of my life to complement their magnificent play. Certainly I have never kicked better, although of course I missed converting both Welsh tries, by Elgan and Jeff Squire. Either would have won us the match. Instead Dusty Hare's three penalties put England on target for the Grand Slam and sent all Welshmen back home to face the recriminations. The post-mortems were still in progress when we played and beat Scotland, a subdued victory and one in which I suffered a hamstring injury which kept me out of the side that played Ireland. It is interesting to reflect that although Wales suffered more than their share of criticism at the time, we scored 20 Championship tries in the two seasons 1979-80, five more than our nearest challengers, Scotland.

In the summer of 1980, it was off to South Africa with the Lions, a short tour for me because of injury. Those that survived the tour, and those that recovered from injury, were then thrust in against New Zealand at the Arms Park in the first of the WRU's special centenary matches. I don't think I've ever played in a Welsh side that was so convincingly beaten in every department, and it occurs to me that the timing of the game, coming so soon after a Lions tour, was asking too much of the players. In any event, I felt ashamed for days afterwards, because the match meant so much to the players and to the public, who had become a little frustrated with the ill-fortune that seemed to be plaguing our game at the time. Some of the damage was repaired, and pride patched up, in the England and Wales versus Scotland and Ireland match, an entertaining frolic which the players and the spectators seemed to enjoy. I mustn't forget Holmesy – he set up the winning try for me, from our own line, in injury time. After the match Jack Young, who had recently retired as a Welsh selector, approached Dai Richards and myself as we supped our pints. After the usual affable greetings, Jack turned to Dai and said: 'Nice to see you back to your best today, David'. It may have been an oblique reference to Dai's failure to score after intercepting against the All Blacks earlier, but Jack really gaffed. Dai hadn't played. He was on the bench. Our centres were Steve Fenwick and Clive Woodward.

Our first Championship match of 1981 was against England at the Arms Park and is known as the one Dusty Hare lost because he failed to kick a last-minute penalty. I prefer to think it was the one which Brynmor Williams, on his debut, won for us with a subtle dummy (he claims) from the base of the scrum which earned a penalty that Steve Fenwick kicked. Fran Cotton went off injured in that match, and it turned out to be his last international.

This paragraph should be bordered in black for it concerns Wales' next and fateful match at Murrayfield. We were hammered and for the backs it was like playing snooker blindfold without the cue ball. For the following match, against Ireland, Dai Richards was the only survivor of the backs who had played at Murrayfield as a result of the most savage piece of surgery inflicted on a Welsh team for some time. We never got the ball, but we certainly got the blame. I felt sorry for myself – but even sorrier that loyal and great servants like J.P.R. Williams and Fenwick should have had their international careers ended so peremptorily and with such little justification.

Sidelined by Wales for the remainder of that season, I was also troubled by a knee injury. An orthopaedic surgeon recommended an operation, and booked me a place in hospital for a fortnight later. Then, suddenly, three days after the diagnosis, I was selected to play for Wales against a World XV. Bad knee or not, I could not resist the chance to play. It was like being capped for the first time all over again. It meant, of course, missing that operation and thank goodness I did, for I was never troubled subsequently. Therefore I was indebted to the selectors, not for picking me, but for saving me from the scalpel.

The wheel completed the circle in December when I was appointed captain of Wales against Australia and for the four Championship matches in 1982. Wales lost three of those matches and we conceded 83 points in the Championship, our worst ever performance in that respect. Scotland beat us 34-18 in the last match, which was the highest score by any visiting side to Wales. My tenuous hopes of staying at the helm, of being part of the inevitable demand for a rebuilt side, faded within a year. I was not only out of the side, but out of the squad. My period in the wilderness became a time for adjustment, for reassessment.

Understandably, I missed being part of the Wales squad during those three years, but perhaps because of it, or maybe despite it, I started to really enjoy my rugby with Cardiff. When eventually I came back into favour in 1985, I had matured in many senses and if the circumstances had been different, and had I had more confidence in myself and in the system, I'm sure I could have done a good job for Wales. I said goodbye not because I didn't want to play for Wales any more, but because I felt I was never going to be more than a stop-gap, no matter how well I played.

I've often asked myself, where did it go wrong? Why did I fail on the odd occasion to fulfil the high expectations others had for me? The answer is not clear-cut, but it is probably due to the fact that I am blithely intuitive, at my best playing off the cuff, relying on instinct to make the right decisions, and I find the stereotyped, set-move game an anathema. When Wales started to move away from individualism towards organised play, I was tangled up in a web of indecision and doubt. When I captained Wales, for instance, I gave too much consideration to events off and on the field. Judgements and decisions which should have been easy suddenly became a cause for concern and sleepless nights. I'm surprised, too, how much I was influenced by the critics' demand for running rugby at all costs when I knew, as sure as night follows day, that this was the formula for disaster in international rugby. Playing so-called attractive rugby and coming second will appeal only momentarily.

Although it sometimes seemed otherwise, international rugby was not the be-all and end-all of my rugby life. There was a lot of fun and pleasure in the 'lesser' matches, the bread-and-butter games with little at stake save personal and team pride. Some you remember with tears, others because they represented at the time a touch of self-indulgence.

It will be easily appreciated that, for instance, my first match for Cardiff, against Penarth in 1974, holds special memories. I remember that I desperately wanted to play well, to impress. It was a tremendous feeling when some of the team came up to me afterwards and said 'well done'.

Three years later, there was Cardiff versus Llanelli in a third round Welsh Cup tie – what a match, what a day. Llanelli, then the supremos of the Cup, led 15-3 at half-time. But we fought back to win 23-15, a great team performance. For me, it was enough to have played well in opposition to Phil Bennett, although a try and a few kicked points were the icing on the cake. As soon as I had changed, I was on the telephone to Tumble RFC. I was eager to know how they had fared against Newport. I don't know what gave me my biggest thrill – Cardiff's win or Tumble's 12-12 draw.

If Cardiff came back from the dead against Llanelli, we gave new meaning to reincarnation against a Barbarian side which contained 14 internationals, in 1976. In those days, there was a Sam Weller-ish element in the Cardiff side and, even though we were trailing 0-24 soon after the start of the second half, we had this preposterous notion that we had the players and the ability to win. There was an incredible atmosphere in that second half as we set about the task. Gareth Edwards set the bandwagon rolling with a try, only for the Baa-Baas to hit back immediately with their fourth try. Not many matches can have been won from such an unpromising situation, but this one was – we scored 25 points in 15 minutes to win 29-28. I don't think I played many better games for Cardiff, and when Edwards dropped the winning goal near the end, I thought the crowd was going to lift the roof off the stand. The Cardiff players were quite pleased, too, not the least our indefatigable skipper, Gerald Davies.

Gerald was the inspiration behind another memorable Cardiff victory, 14-10 against Australia in 1975. I scored a try and two penalties, but what I remember most was a scintillating pre-match team talk from Gerald in the Centre Hotel. It sends shivers down my back just thinking about it. I'm convinced Cardiff would have beaten any side that day, so hyped up were we. It's fascinating to recall, too, that for that match Brynmor Williams came in as a last-minute replacement for Gareth Edwards and sitting on the bench was a pale-faced, gaunt youngster named Holmes.

Cardiff have a marvellous record against Australia. We always seem to produce our best against them. This was certainly so in 1984, when we outplayed what was virtually their Test team. It was a very good performance and it looked even better when set in comparison with what the Aussies did to Wales a little later on in the tour.

No-one has yet convinced me of the reasons why Cup finals are often disappointing. I have taken part in four finals with Cardiff – three victories and one defeat – and I don't think we played well in one of them. It is easy to understand how Pontypool felt after they were criticised for the way they played to beat Swansea in 1983 – in the final analysis it seems that all that matters in a Cup final is winning it.

It is curious therefore that some of our best matches have been in the early rounds of the Cup. Cardiff certainly haven't played better or with more purpose than we did when beating Pontypool in the 1985 semi-final at Newport. They had thrashed us a fortnight earlier, and they were obvious favourites to beat us again. But we really got our act together on the day. Not many sides can claim that they have outplayed 'Pooler', and personally I regard that win as one of the finest in my period with Cardiff. There should be no confusion about it, either. It wasn't a matter of Pontypool having an off-day. We had planned how we would play and we carried out our game strategy with precision. We simply refused to allow them to play their game. The domination, fore and aft, was Cardiff's.

I have played in over 300 matches for Cardiff since I joined them in 1974, and, allowing for a few tepid performances, I am rather glad to say that only once did I play really badly. It was against Bath in 1982. We were hammered. I had a dreadful afternoon, completely draining. I was so bad in fact that I nearly decided to quit rugby altogether. Fortunately, wise counsel and friendly advice from the lads encouraged me to think again and eventually to abandon a decision that I would have regretted for the rest of my life.

'A man loves and admires his own country
because it produced him'

Anon

3
TUMBLE

Although I now live, with my wife Helen and three-year-old daughter Kathryn Elizabeth, in one of Cardiff's fashionable outlying districts, almost under the shadow of the historic Llandaff Cathedral, my home in most other senses is Tumble, a small village in West Wales. Straddling a hill, Tumble consists of two communities, the people living at the top comprising Upper Tumble and those at the other end Lower Tumble. Not that a visitor would notice the difference: travelling through the village, he would only have to blink and he would be through Tumble – Lower, Middle and Upper – before his eyes had re-opened. He could be in Llanelli (seven miles away) or Carmarthen (11 miles in the other direction) without even realising that he had just missed the second largest village in Wales – just a dot on the map. Tumble's obscurity seems to be sufficient reason for me to try to give it a geographical identity, to describe its character and relate some of its history.

I was born at the bottom, as it were, in Lower Tumble, in a council house on the Rhosnewydd estate in Bethesda Road. I moved up in the world, geographically speaking, in 1961 when I was five and we moved to Upper Tumble, where for the princely sum of £300 my father, Elvet, bought a semi-detached house in Heol y Bryn. The move was not so much a bettering of the lot or the outlook of the Davies household as a desire to keep the Heol y Bryn house in the family for it had originally belonged to my great-grandfather. He had bought the land in 1900 but the house was not completed until 1902, the same year as the Ebenezer Chapel down the hill, which you can see, square and solid in good old Welsh stone, from our back living-room window. Three hundred pounds was a pretty good price for a property in those days – a sound investment, as any National & Provincial Building Society manager would tell you. It is still home to me because my parents still live there, Mam making tea and tendering Welsh cakes to friends and strangers and Dad, when suitably provoked, proffering home-spun philosophy.

As I have said Tumble is small, not much more than one road with a few houses and streets sprigging from it. Architecturally, the village would have more appeal to Gren, the *South Wales Echo* cartoonist, than Alec Clifton-Taylor, though its very ordinariness has a reassuring quality about it. If it is different in any way it is that it is hemmed in on all sides by rolling, hilly countryside, where farms, fields and smallholdings are reminders of what life was like there before the geologists uncovered the wealth beneath. Today there are still chapels, of course, a working men's club, one pub (the Tumble Hotel), a fish and chip shop, a barber's, a chemist's, two banks (Lloyd's and Midland) and the rugby club itself, which steadfastly remains the social centre of the community. The club's large function room would be the envy of many senior clubs, and has been the venue for many a convivial event, from banquets to concerts. There's more bingo than Bach nowadays, I have to confess.

As do so many houses in so many villages in Wales, 31 Heol y Bryn – a solid, brick-built three-up three-down dwelling – presents a modest, unpretentious face to the world. The front door opens on to a narrow pavement and then the street, and traffic, though there is precious little of that these days. The garden at the back is comparatively large – 70 yards long. It is also an oddity, for it starts 20 feet below our ground floor and slopes even further downwards thereafter. Looking back up the incline from Dad's lines of cabbages, an impression is gained of a split level house, which Heol y Bryn most certainly is not. Nor was the garden any use whatsoever for cricket or tennis – you'd literally be bowling uphill. It is, however, still an activity centre for an underground working man, as my father was, where he can potter among the vegetables and flowers and breathe in clean, fresh air. When I was a boy most other residents of Heol y Bryn, whether they lived in a semi, detached or terraced house, depended for their livelihood on coal. It's different now. It's dole not coal. Tumble's pits have gone and the only anthracite dust that remains is that which scars the lungs of old miners.

Our move up the hill in 1961 took place a year before the closure of Tumble's last great natural resource, Mynydd Mawr, or in English, Great Mountain, a mine which produced some of the finest anthracite in the Welsh coalfields. Although there are a few privately owned shallow drift mines still operating, the death of Great Mountain marked the last rites of Tumble as a major coal producer. There are still miners there, of course, but they are only a handful compared with the hundreds employed in Great Mountain's 80-year history. It is odd, in a way, to think that a hole in the ground provided the backbone of a village's economy and was responsible for its transformation in the last century from an isolated rural community. Most of the few remaining working miners claw the glistening, black gold from the earth below Cynheidre, six miles down the road. Those that do not work underground have scant choice of local employment. Either they work in a small factory which makes window blinds, or sign on, those two dreadful words so redolent of even harsher times in the 1920s.

For some of those who have stayed on, memories of those bad old days are still etched deep. You have only to talk to an old miner, or his family, and you can feel the resentment, the anger, an almost tangible bitterness. For the younger generation, the running down of the economy has been at best depressing, at worst devastating. For those, like myself, drawn away by career demands, the occasional return to Tumble is a mixture of eager anticipation of going home and profound sadness that I am a helpless outsider witnessing the decline. Much better, one thinks, to look on the brighter side, to be optimistic. There's Mam's cooking, jawing with life-long pals and socialising in the club – all agreeable diversions from the comparatively frenetic lifestyle of Cardiff. It's always good to go home. It is curious but nonetheless true that absence from one's birthplace invariably increases one's appreciation of it. I have learned much more about Tumble, I think, since I left than I knew when it was the cradle of my ambition. In my days of short-trousered innocence, I readily admit I was pre-occupied far more with normal youthful athletic pursuits than with the turbulent history of Tumble. Cricket and rugby seemed more relevant than culture and religion, even though they were not really approved of by my father.

Despite various influences and 'foreign' invasions over the years, the village has remained singularly Welsh in character, culture and language. It could almost represent in microcosm the Welsh experience which has left its mark upon us all. Both burdened and enriched by the Industrial Revolution, and strident in radicalism and religion, the village would have been odd if it had not embraced the most Welsh tradition of them all rugby football. English speculators, Bristolian labourers and craftsmen – Scots too – came to Tumble to make fortune and fame from coal and the railway. T. Nefyn Williams and L. Rowe Williams, hot gospellers of their day, stoked up my ancestors with passionate eloquence from the pulpit, and the mountain-top and meeting-hall oratory of the likes of Enoch Rees, William Abraham (Mabon), S.O. Davies, Daniel Walters and, later, Lady Megan Lloyd George, James Griffiths and Gwynoro Jones stirred the political consciousness of Tumble folk. The speculators have come and gone, Great Mountain pit is sealed and silent, the old railway track to Llanelli stretches desolate in a shroud of weed and grass, the pubs are boarded and padlocked, and the chapels, unused for six days a week and half-empty on the seventh, echo other disillusionments.

The sad, languid side of Tumble is not the whole picture, of course. Cheery and cheerful, good natured and good humoured, the Welsh cope marvellously with adversity. And when all else seems black and doleful, there is always the game to lift spirits, get hearts thumping and set in motion that endless cycle of argument, debate and comment which is the life-blood of a community that has little else to enthuse over. Rugby is inextricably woven into the fabric of most Welsh village societies. Tumble is no exception.

In this context I may be forgiven for suggesting that the person who perhaps made the most enduring impression on Tumble society was one Thiophilous Evans, acknowledged founder of Tumble RFC, my first club. There is a picture of Thiophilous in the clubhouse, but I have to plead biographical ignorance about Ophie, as he became known, except that he bought a rugby ball out of his own pocket-money, cajoled friends into helping him form a side and was appointed the club's first ever captain in 1897. Successive generations of Tumbleites owe Ophie much, for without the rugby club the youth of the village might have been hard pressed to have found other outlets for their leisure time.

This is best exemplified by the story of Archie Skym, a redoubtable forward who played for Wales 20 times between 1928 and 1935. Archie has always been regarded as Tumble's first international player, a fondly held view which disregards his disqualification: he was born in Drefach, just up the road. What is unquestionable is that Archie learned his rugby in Tumble. A local miner, he first played the game 'for something to do' during the National Coal Strike in 1926. He is a true Tumble player in that respect. By all accounts, Archie was a magnificent forward, hard, strong and committed. He played in Wales' Championship-winning side in 1931 and in the much-lauded side which triumphed at Twickenham for the first time in 1933. Archie, along with the captain Watcyn Thomas, was the veteran of that 1933 side which included, among seven new caps, Messrs Wilf Wooller and Vivian Jenkins, both of whom in their subsequent journalistic careers were more than kind in their criticism of my play when I started my international career. Perhaps they remembered that Archie, one of those whose performances helped make their debuts so memorable, had also been a Tumble player.

As it happens my links with Archie Skym are even closer than our rugby origins. By uncommon coincidence, his playing career 50 years ago was an exact precursor of mine, for he too played for Tumble, Llanelli, Cardiff and Wales in that order, and we both were honoured by the captaincy of Cardiff. There were differences in our curricula vitae: Archie missed going to Oxford University, I was not invited to join the South Glamorgan Constabulary. I was four when Archie died in Cardiff, aged 63. It is fascinating to recall that Archie had the distinction of playing for Wales in the front row, second row and back row, which must be unique for an international player.

More recently, of course, the great Denzil Williams and Neath's Brian Thomas played prop and lock for Wales, but I suspect the only player who approached Archie's remarkable achievement was another Llanelli forward, Emrys Evans. Emrys played his first match for Wales in his accustomed position of prop, against England in 1937, but when recalled in 1939 he was required to do duty against Scotland and Ireland as flanker, a position in which he had never played at the time of his selection. The experience of Skym and Evans certainly seems to put modern selection eccentricities in perspective.

It is something of a Welsh pastime for clubs, particularly junior ones, to claim that such and such an international played for them. Evidence of the link between club and player is often tenuous. Who am I to spoil the fun and ruin a thousand anecdotal stories? Fortunately, as far as Tumble is concerned, we have little reason to resort to apocrypha: apart from myself, only one other player born and bred in Tumble went on to play international rugby. Des Jones was born in the village in 1925 and was a miner at Great Mountain. A lock forward, his contribution to Tumble's fortunes was recognised when he was selected by West Wales against Aberavon. Tumble may well have had cause to regret Des's elevation to representative rugby, for Aberavon were so impressed with his play they invited him to join them, which he did. Two seasons a Wizard, he became a Scarlet in 1947 and a Welsh player a year later. As Archie Skym had done before him, Des switched from mining to the police.

Apart from our birthplace, Des and I share another intriguing connection. His father, known as Wil Ardwyn, who came from Aberystwyth, played alongside my grandfather, Dai Davies, in the Tumble side during the First World War. Many clubs disbanded during the war years, for obvious reasons. Tumble, like other clubs in mining areas, continued to play because many of their players were exempted from call-up. Some took advantage of the exemption and returned from other activities to the pits to avoid the daily slaughter in the trenches. One who came back was Evan Davies, known as Ianto Penygraig, who, after playing wing for Llanelli and gaining a Welsh trial, had signed professionally 'for £250 down' for Oldham in 1911. Ianto returned to Tumble and was allowed to play amateur rugby because of the WRU wartime amnesty. According to my father the tales of Ianto's rugby exploits were legion. When he signed for Oldham, Llanelli lost 'the cleverest wing in Wales'.

'Ianto was the greatest ever player up there in the North', my father claims. 'He was like a god and he was treated like one.'

Apparently, Ianto played marvellously at Tumble too, his party piece being an ability to leap over a combined scrummage (shades of Lynn Davies!). Sadly, Ianto ended up in a wheelchair, ravaged by arthritis. In later years, despite his handicap, Ianto loved a visit to the Tumble Hotel for a pint with his pals. 'He used to play darts from his wheelchair,' says Dad, 'and I can tell you his opponent had to be good to beat him.'

Ianto Penygraig was never an international Rugby Union player, although he did tour with the Great Britain League side to Australia in 1920. Tumble can boast other players who have played for them and for Wales. Peter Rees and Handel Greville, now luminaries on Llanelli's committee, who were capped in 1947, wore Tumble's black and white hoops, Rees captaining the club in 1952-53, after his retirement from first-class rugby.

Tumble's pride in their association with five international players may be reflected glory but it is understandable nevertheless, for after all they are only a village club and a small one at that. Personally, I have many reasons to be grateful to them. When I was capped for the first time, against Australia in Brisbane in 1978, I received, if my memory serves me well, 17 congratulatory telegrams. One of these was from Tumble RFC, and it will remain a treasured possession for it confirmed that my first club and my home village wanted to share in one of the most memorable moments of my career:

To 9.20 AM JUN 9 '78
GARETH DAVIES
WELSH RUGBY UNION
CREST INTERNATIONAL HOTEL
BRISBANE

HEARTIEST CONGRATULATIONS AND ALL THE VERY BEST FOR THE BIG MATCH

TUMBLE RUGBY FOOTBALL CLUB

Various theories have been advanced as to the derivation of Tumble's name. The most persistent and probably the most widely believed is that it stems from the position of the village on a hillside. This explanation was offered, I believe, by Dr Melville Richards, in a series of broadcasts on Welsh place-names in 1964 – rocks tumbling down from the top and so forth.

Much more plausible, if less flattering, is that Tumble owes its name to Oliver Cromwell's son, Richard. The Protector's son earned the sobriquet of Tumbledown Dick, after his much derided failure to stand firmly in his appointed duties. And, according to the custom of the time, many inns and public houses were named 'The Tumbledown Dick' after Richard's political demise in 1659. There is evidence that an inn existed in Tumble in the 1800s, perhaps even earlier, and it is conceivable that this too was called 'The Tumbledown Dick' and that the Welsh name for the village, 'Y Tymbl', was familiarly derived from the anglicised name. It is interesting that in 1907 Llannon Parish Council, who were responsible for Tumble's affairs, unanimously passed the proposal 'that the present name of the village called Tumble be changed and called from henceforth Arfryn, and the clerk may inform the Chief Postmaster'. ('Arfryn', roughly translated, means top of the hill.) If the Council's idea is suggestive of a local desire to re-establish their Welshness, it is perhaps an understandable reaction to the growing influence of English industrialists and speculators, who had moved into the area to exploit the earth's wealth and by association the local inhabitants. However, the motive for the change in name has never been satisfactorily explained; nor indeed was it adopted. Tumble it was, Tumble it still is.

Whether or not the Tumble Inn played a part in the foundation of the village, it certainly featured prominently in Tumble's formative affairs, sometimes in unusual ways. Before the completion of the Baptist Chapel in 1890, prayer meetings were regularly held in the Inn's long room. A year earlier, an auction was held in the Inn for the sale of an adjoining house and land. The auctioneer's blurb read: 'a large colliery has been opened within 100 yards or so of the house, and the district is rapidly improving so much that property of all kinds is improving very much in value'. This may refer to the earliest workings of the Great Mountain seams and graphically illustrates the attitudes of the day. Coal meant profit for some, employment for others, and they came in their hundreds from near and far to work, live and give the village its identity. At the Tumble Inn auction, William Phillips, a merchant from Llanelli, paid £50 for the house and land with the intention of establishing a shop to supply the growing population. Shortly afterwards he changed his mind, and re-sold the property to a group of local people, who wanted to erect a Baptist Chapel. Mr Phillips made a profit of four pounds on the deal and Tumble had its first religious building.

Up to then, the villagers had had to make do and mend when it came to religion, which was, of course, the bedrock of Welsh culture as the Industrial Revolution changed the face of the country. The fire of the great religious revival in Wales led by Evan Roberts, the miner-lay preacher, had yet to be lit when Tumble believers, having no baptistry, undertook remarkable improvisation. Presumably following New Testament guidelines, they carried out baptismal ceremonies in nearby rivers and streams.

There were, as I've said, prayers and pints side by side in the Tumble Inn, and an even more equivocal attitude to the evils of drink was manifested by the deal the local vicar struck with Buckley's Brewery. The Brewery, situated at Felinfoel, piped up the water to Great Mountain Working Men's Club, and readily acceded to a request by the minister of the day, L. Rowe Williams, that their supply be tapped: 'The Bethel Trustees shall be at liberty to tap the water supply of the Company . . . at such a spot as shall be pointed out to them by the Company, to take water therefrom by means of a line of pipes and hydrant, such water to be used solely for baptismal purposes at the Bethel Baptist Chapel. The Trustees shall pay to the Company the sum of one shilling per annum'.

Although my parents are no longer the chapel-going regulars that they and their parents used to be, they still relate with pride that my great-grandfather was a founder deacon of the Ebenezer Chapel, which was built in 1900. The Methodists certainly played their part in early Tumble society, none more so than T. Nefyn Williams, one of their ministers. Nefyn Williams knew how to stir things up, apparently, and his non-belief in the Trinity and oft-expressed doubts about the Virgin Birth made him a sort of Bishop of Durham of his day. He also related his ministry to the community in which he lived, adapting the Communion Service, for instance, by bringing to communicants a lump of coal on a plate instead of bread and wine.

Another character of the district was my great-great-grandfather, known locally as Twm Casken Bach. A farmer, he used to supplement his income by delivering beer by horse and cart from the Gwendraeth Brewery to the surrounding farms. Twm had to be careful, apparently, where he watered the horses, for he was often at risk of losing his load to footpads who would lay in wait for him. There could be no case of mistaken identity either. Great-great-granddad, six foot one, thin as a rake and toothless, always wore a bowler hat. My mother remembers him tethering the horses outside our house and popping in for a cup of tea. 'That bowler hat always stayed on' she says. 'He never took it off, even when he was sitting down to eat.'

The coming of the railway to Tumble in 1880 was an important event. It was laid down by John Waddell, a Scotsman who is better known as the builder of the Mersey Tunnel and

Putney Bridge. The Llanelli & Mynydd Mawr Railway took the coal out, for sale all over the world, and brought in more workers to the steadily growing village. Coal, of course, was at the heart of all things in Tumble, and it meant different things to different people. My father spent 36 years down the pit, first Great Mountain, then Blaenurwen and Cynheidre. His love-hate relationship with coal started 51 years ago, when he was 14. He worked six days a week for 13s 10d, not enough he'd say to buy even a pint of bitter today, but a valuable contribution to the Davies household in the days of hardship and poverty before the Second World War. Every penny mattered. Today Da' Tumble, as my daughter Kathryn affectionately calls him, will pick up a lump of anthracite, familiarly touching its hardness and admiring its diamond-like shine, and say: 'It's a pity they can't find some other use for it. It's far too good to burn'.

Yet it's that same coal which has ravaged his health. One of the more ghastly memories of my youth was to watch as this strong, sturdily-built man coughed and gasped for breath, another victim of the awful lung affliction which has sent many a miner to an early grave. He cannot grip or form a fist with his left hand, which was mangled in a conveyor back in 1967. The scars are criss-crossed, blue and black, like the work of some demented tattooist.

If my father has an ambivalent attitude to coal it is understandable. A thoughtful, sensitive and private person – traits which I believe I've inherited – he keeps much to himself these days. But when I was a boy he told me of the depredation which followed the Coal Strike in the 1920s, comparing it with the famous Tumble Strike of 1893 when the Llanelli police aided by the Inniskillen Dragoons enforced the Riot Act against the local miners. He is not bitter about the fact that most of his life has been one of struggle and labour, except in that the all-consuming work of a miner inhibited travel and opportunity.

'You worked so hard, you were so tired you couldn't even go up to Llannon. That was another world, and it was just up the road. We knew nothing about it, nothing about the people or anything, or anywhere else. Tumble and our village was our world, the only one we knew.'

His own bitter-sweet experience of mining further fashioned his ideas and his philosophy. He is contemptuous of the last Coal Strike, led by Arthur Scargill.

'It was nonsensical' he argues. 'That's the truth. They were supposed to be fighting to keep the pits open. In my view the sooner they all close the better. It's a bloody pity they ever opened in the first place.'

He has never told me what he would have liked to have been, had he had the opportunity of being anything other than a miner. Perhaps a doctor. Or an architect. One profession he certainly would not have followed is that of a sportsman. Which is another way of saying he never did approve of the path I took . . .

'Ymmob Braint y Mae Dyledswydd'
In every honour there is responsibility
Gwendraeth Grammar School motto

4
GWENDRAETH

Carwyn James once wrote: 'William Gareth Davies was born, bred and schooled to captain Wales'. Coming from a former pupil at my old school, Gwendraeth Grammar, Carwyn's remarks could well have invited a charge of nepotism, or 'a bit o' bias' as we say in West Wales. Being a sucker for flattery – and being ambitious in the direction pointed out by Carwyn anyway – naturally I savoured his opinion, particularly as it came from the pen of a man much revered throughout Wales for his perspicacity, knowledge and original thought. The trouble was, Carwyn hadn't got it quite right. His views were based on assumptions, wrong ones because in two respects at least I didn't qualify. I was neither born nor bred to play rugby, let alone to captain Wales. I'm not even sure I was schooled for such an honour either.

Carwyn presumed that like most Welsh boys I was reared in an environment where rugby transcended all, and playing for Wales was on a par with landing on the moon, climbing Everest or swimming the Atlantic. It wasn't that such hopes were considered unattainable in our house – they were simply not on the curriculum. Elvet Davies's priorities, as far as his son was concerned, centred on academic qualifications which would lead to a 'respectable' profession. Understandably, perhaps, after his own hard life down the pits, he had decided that the only way that I could avoid a similar fate lay in education, in studying hard and by so doing getting more of a chance than he had had. Sport was only to be tolerated as light relief, which is another way of saying that he was steadfast in never wanting me to play rugby – or any sport for that matter –

if it was going to interfere with his expectations. I have to admit I found it hard to comply with such an ostensibly rigid regime, and being something of a 'sports nut' as a boy, I had to resort more than once to a little bit of subterfuge to have the best of both worlds. My co-conspirator was my mother, who worked on the principle that what my father didn't see, he didn't have to know about. I lost count of the number of occasions I sneaked past him as he read his paper or dozed, raced out into the garden where Mam would throw down my kit to me from a bedroom window. I was away, like a thief in the night, and Dad hadn't an inkling that I'd gone. My 'escapes' were, of course, not always successful. Whenever he found out, usually the next day, that I'd gone off to play cricket or rugby somewhere, I'd get hell. Many was the time I skulked off to bed, in tears, thinking how unfair life was. Having said that, my father really did nothing positive to dampen my athletic enthusiasm, nor did he try to hinder what progress I made. There were no threats of cutting off my pocket money, no cuffs across the ear, just lectures on the triviality of sport. I learned of the dangers of misspent youth often.

Mam, I assume, retained a more usual Welsh attitude to sport: if you were kicking a rugby ball about the field, you were less likely to get into mischief. (There is a lot to be said for that philosophy in a wider sense, and I'm a firm believer in the character-building aspect of sport.) Not that everything I did gained Mam's approval. Once, when I was 11, I came home late from school with the seat of my new long trousers covered in mud. Mam seemed reasonably appeased when I explained. That day Barry John and Gareth Edwards had come to Gwendraeth for a practice session. I had stayed behind to watch them and found myself the only boy left, standing behind the goal-posts to collect the balls as they kicked. My 'job' was to collect the ball and kick it back to them, and that would have been fine, but for the fact that in taking the first kick from B.J. I slipped and fell flat on my back in the mud. So much for showing up in front of one's heroes.

Eventually, my involvement and interest in sporting activities became a matter of acquiescence, even indifference on Dad's part, something which I did not like, but which was certainly better than being told I couldn't play. As a consequence, sport was only rarely discussed at home, but because I was reasonably successful in an academic sense, probably Dad was grudgingly satisfied that his wishes and aspirations were still seemingly being fulfilled. With Mam skimping to ensure I would always have a new pair of boots, or shorts, or cricket gloves, I realise how lucky I was. I was certainly no deprived child. If I did miss out in any way when I was a lad, it was just, I suppose, that my father never once said 'well done' if I achieved any distinction at cricket, athletics or rugby. This apparent detachment probed at my sensitivity, and often puzzled me, and partly explains why we have remained distant from each other.

It was many years in fact before I began fully to appreciate my father's point of view, and what was important to me as a boy seems now rather less so. It was only recently too that I discovered that far from being oblivious to my sporting attainments, he meticulously kept records and cuttings. It is strange that he never told me what he was doing, or of his covert interest. But that's the way he is, quaintly secretive and introspective, a man hard to know, a man who keeps his emotions under wraps. In understanding what sort of person he is, I have also come to accept the reason for the most curious of all his whims – that in the 20-odd years I have been playing rugby, and cricket, he has never once seen me play.

For many years I was convinced the explanation lay in an incident which took place way back at Tumble Primary School, on Sports Day, when I was seven or eight. Nature had invested me with a little more speed than most of my schoolmates. I was expected by everyone to win most of the foot races. Halfway through the afternoon, I lined up for the start of one dash when I spotted my father standing with other parents some distance away. I had had no idea that he was coming to watch and to this day, I do not know what happened. 'Ready . . . Steady . . . Go', everyone raced away, leaving me like a spot on a domino. I found I could not move. I had frozen on the start-line, petrified. As everyone shouted the boys to the line, I peered again towards my father. The anguished look on his face told its own story – he had decided my 'disgrace' was entirely his fault, that I had seized up for no other reason than that he was there, watching me. He never came to watch me again, and I was sure I knew why until quite recently when I learned the real reason. As a boy, he used to be a fair cricketer and rugby player. But whenever his father went along to watch him, inevitably he'd be out first ball, or he'd drop every pass thrown to him. He says: 'When it happened to Gareth, just the same way, I decided it would be better for both of us if I didn't go along to watch him'. He is certainly a man of his word – though I'm sure he's had a sneak look at the television whenever I've been on. He might not admit to it though.

With his attitude, it is hardly surprising that my father rarely treated me to a day out at a sports event. In fact the last time he did so was 23 March 1968 when he took me to watch Wales play France at Cardiff Arms Park. I was 11 years old, and thrilled by the prospect of watching my idols, Barry John included, give the French a lesson. Oh, the glowing optimism of youth. Wales had already lost to Ireland and drawn with England, but surely the French, already champions with three wins out of three, would be eclipsed, their dreams of a first-ever Grand Slam laid waste by the power of the Welsh pack and the artistry and cunning of B.J. and Gareth Edwards? So much for cherished hopes. It was a ghastly day, in more ways than one. The rain slashed down, it was cold and miserable, and it was Wales, surrendering a 9-3 lead, who finally gave way to the control and experience of the Camberabero brothers, Lilian and Guy. I suppose I should have felt privileged to have seen them, those two fine French half-backs, particularly as this was their last international. I'm afraid I didn't. My father and I stood, soaked to the skin, in the East terrace as they steered France into the history books. Disconsolate, chilled and wet, I cried as Dad yanked me through the crowds at the end, towards the railway station. Never had I felt so dejected. Dad wasn't very happy either. My tears seemed to make him even more churlish. 'I'll never take you to a match again', he threatened. He never did.

Later, when I was big enough and brave enough to go to matches on my own, and Carwyn James among others was predicting an international career for me, Dad changed tack. He became critical, particularly if I'd had a bad game or the Press were less than their usual kind selves. 'Ach', he'd say, 'Forget it. You'll never play for Wales.' As I've said, Carwyn was a bit awry with that 'born and bred' bit . . .

Now my mother was an altogether different type of person. Whenever she could, she'd make the effort to go to a match. The trouble was, I'd get her a ticket and she wouldn't watch, which probably suggests the Davies were a very strange family indeed – Father not wanting a ticket and not going to a match, Mother eager for a ticket, but not using it. Mam's eccentricity first showed itself when I played for Welsh Schools against Welsh Youth at the Brewery Field, Bridgend, in 1974. She watched for a few moments and then spent the rest of the match either in the tea-room or walking around the ground. It was the same thing at Twickenham, at the 'Varsity Match in 1977, at my Championship debut Scotland versus Wales at Murrayfield in 1979, and at several other matches at Cardiff. By the end, Mam had become the world's leading authority on the outside of grounds. She'd never explain her enigmatic perambulations. Possibly she was apprehensive of seeing her little boy getting hurt, or perhaps she was frightened of the noise, the bustle of the crowds inside the grounds. A bit different, she'd say, from shopping at the Co-op at Cross Hands. Later on, she made a habit of coming to see me before matches in the team hotel at Cardiff, to wish me luck and to give Terry Holmes a bag of Welsh cakes. Terry had once come to tea at Tumble and remarked favourably on the quality of Mam's Welsh cakes. He couldn't have made a nicer remark. She pressed Welsh cakes on him from then on, and it became a sort of ritual before matches. Terry even had to take some to France on one occasion. It was a silly sort of gesture, really, but I loved Mam for it. And so did Terry.

Maybe the Davies household were not so mad, or unusual really. I read once that Bobby and Jack Charlton's father wasn't over enamoured with football, their passion, and hardly ever watched them play. He preferred boxing apparently. And then there was Chris Lloyd's father. He did come to see her play Martina Navratilova in the 1985 Wimbledon final, but this is something he rarely does because he always ends up a nervous wreck whenever he watches her play. Another interesting contrast concerns Mark Hughes, the Manchester United and Wales player. His number one fan is his mother. She hardly ever misses an opportunity to go to cheer him on.

Looking back, I suppose the topsy-turvy attitudes I experienced at home could easily have affected mine towards the game. Instead, they seemed to fuel my ambition and determination to succeed. It seems I've spent my life trying to prove something or other. Being part of the rugby set-up at Gwendraeth Grammar, and the Tumble club, certainly helped in this respect, for in both I found support and encouragement which counted for a great deal later on.

Gwendraeth is noted as a breeding ground for leading rugby players, and for the school to have produced ten pupils who have played for Wales is an achievement which must compare favourably with that of any similarly sized educational establishment in a relatively remote rural area. Yet, harking back again to Carwyn's pronouncement, the rugby influence there was more superficial than one might imagine. For most of my time at Gwendraeth, for instance, we could hardly have been thought of as living and breathing the game for, apart from house matches, rarely did we play more than two or three matches against other schools in a season. And when we did, in my early days at least, we got trounced so often that few of us coveted ambitions of playing in the so-called big-time. Not many of us thought we'd make it.

Nevertheless Gwendraeth has some claims to being one of Max Boyce's fly-half factories. When Jonathan Davies was capped against England at the end of the 1985 season, he was the fourth fly-half from the school to wear the Wales jersey, succeeding myself, Barry John and Carwyn James. Ken Jones played occasionally at stand-off at school, and at Llanelli, but it was at centre that he played for Wales. Not all Gwendraeth's products were maestros of the midfield. Luther Morgan (the first former pupil to be capped, in 1938) and Des Jones were forwards, Peter Rees and Robert Morgan were wings, and Handel Greville was a scrum-half. Handel, Carwyn, B.J. and myself, all half-backs, had another thing in common – we each won our first cap against Australia. Jonathan spoiled things a bit by getting his against England.

I've been asked many times how much I was influenced by Gwendraeth's great traditions in producing players with flair. The truth is, very little. I can honestly say no-one actually *taught* me how to play, for instance how to give and take a pass, or kick, or beat a man. Apart from what people call natural ball skills, most of what I learned was from trying to emulate others. I practised a lot, and the encouragement I received from say, someone like Ray Williams, our school coach, was important. It wasn't teaching, or coaching, in the exact sense. In fact coaching passed me by, or at least I did not become involved with it until I was part of the Welsh Schools set-up. The point was, coaching was not imposed upon me, it was not a strict regime, and I think I benefited from being generally allowed to play my own game.

I do not want to denigrate Ray Williams' role in those formative years, during which ideas are fashioned and help direct you later. As a wing, Ray probably did not feel qualified to instruct in fly-half skills, and what he did do was to try to keep alive my interest in the game. I have come across far worse communicators, and I believe now he was artful in his psychology. He tried many a subtle artifice to kindle my enthusiasm. He recognised that youngsters are very responsive to praise. They like being told they have done well. I was no exception. When I was 12, for instance, Ray was particularly effusive after one house match in which I had scored a good try, running in from 40 yards. 'You keep on playing like this,' he told me, 'and you'll be better than Barry John.' I puffed with pride, even more eager to 'prove' myself, which, of course, is what Ray had had in mind. There was no doubt, either, that I became his blue-eyed boy at school and that my conditioning for the future took place as much in discussion off the field as in action on it. I remember once grumbling about a long journey we had to undertake to play a match (in those days Aberystwyth, 35 miles away, seemed like the other side of the world). Said Ray: 'you know, when you're playing for Llanelli and you've got to travel to places like London or Coventry or Northampton, you've got to be able to adjust to long journeys'. It was another piece of Ray's kidology, but it was also something more. It was evidence of his assumption that one day I'd be playing for Llanelli, a perfectly natural progression for a West Walian schoolboy who wanted to play first-class rugby. In Ray's mind, no other club existed. Or mattered. As it happened, he was preaching to the converted. I had long set my heart on becoming a Scarlet. That there might one day be a choice of clubs never entered my head, nor did I question the parish-pump attitude that governed my young life. I was going to be a Llanelli player, and that was that.

School rugby, as I've intimated, wasn't the be-all and end-all for me. Part of the reason was that, for most of the time, I didn't really enjoy it, particularly the defeats. Once, against Llandovery College, we were hammered 60-0. I was 13 and ended the match with stitches in my head after being kicked when I tried to make a low tackle and failed. Who knows, perhaps that was the explanation for, or at least the start of, my reputation for being an if, but and maybe tackler. If I learned a lesson against Llandovery, I learned another at 15, when Gwendraeth were playing at home against Pontyberem High School. Neither side was very good, but we usually beat them, and this may have been in the referee's mind during the match. Apart from being the Pontyberem PE teacher, Thomas 'Gym', the referee, was a selector for the district representative XV, Mynydd Mawr Schools. Important, see. Anyway, Mr Thomas was clearly showing Pontyberem undue favour, at least I thought so. After a while, I could restrain myself no longer. 'You are a cheat', I declared most unadvisedly. 'Don't talk to me like that or you won't be picked for Mynydd Mawr', I was warned forcefully. My second mistake was to think that a PE teacher wouldn't be able to spell taxidermist let alone know what it meant, and my reply earned the dreaded pointed finger. I was sent off. That was when the world really fell about my ears. Oh, the shame, the scandal, fancy being sent off, bringing the school into disrepute. I was given the most severe dressing-down of my life by Ray Williams and other teachers. I wished I could have crawled through a crack in the floor-boards when Alan Stone, my form master, rollicked me in front of everyone. Davies the Gab became Davies Trap-shut from that moment on.

That incident apart, I was usually on good terms with the masters at Gwendraeth. I had a lot of respect for Les 'Biol' Jones, from Brynamman. No patroniser he, and if to many he was a little prim and proper, he taught me much in the way of courtesy and self-respect. Another teacher whom I liked was Eifion 'Maths' Thomas, but for another reason. He loved rugby and he loved talking about it even more. It was always a joy to be in his company, even when, taking some extra-curricular Maths lessons on Sunday mornings, the class-room was the Cross Hands Working Men's Club. Eifion liked his Sunday pint. Sad to say, despite Eifion's help I failed my 'A' Level Maths, which didn't go down very well at home, as Maths was a subject beloved of my father. My explanation for the failure was unconvincing, I remember. I kept quiet the fact that I'd been playing cricket the day before the exam when revision might have served me far better.

I enjoyed my Youth cricket very much, and playing for Welsh Secondary Schools was on a par with winning my first schoolboy rugby cap, which may surprise some people. There are many examples of rugby players excelling at both codes, notably Dusty Hare in recent years. By comparison, my cricket career was a modest one. I played once for Glamorgan Seconds, which was a marvellous experience, but events steered me away from seriously considering it as a main-line activity. Now had golf been my summer sport, that might have been a different thing . . . Gwendraeth meant many other things to me, of course, and not the least was that it was where I met my wife, Helen. Very romantic it was too, that first encounter – we dissected a rat together in the lab.

If I had one disappointment at Gwendraeth it was that I never became Head Boy. That was the result, I suppose, of being so involved in sport. My sport as a boy wasn't confined to school. I joined Tumble RFC Youth team, and over the years played far more for the village club than I did for Gwendraeth. If I have fond memories of that time, and they were great days, it is not only because I remember the fun, the matches and the friendships I made at Tumble RFC. It may seem a paltry gesture to some, but Tumble were tremendously supportive of me as a boy and whenever I played at representative level, whether it was cricket or rugby, they always made it their business to ensure I had sufficient funds for expenses. Often it wasn't much, but it meant a great deal to me, and gave me an independence I might not otherwise have enjoyed. The financial help did not stop when I left West Wales. When I went up to Oxford in 1977 I found I couldn't afford such things as blazers, sweaters and ties, and again Tumble came to the rescue. The most munificent contribution, however, came when I faced, penniless as usual in those days, the tour to Australia with Wales in 1978. Many major wealthy clubs support their players on overseas tours, but it is fantastic that a small club like Tumble should do so, and I was overwhelmed when they presented me with the proceeds of a club dance they had staged specially for the purpose. Whatever happens in the future in the higher reaches of the game, no matter how professional it might become, it is gratifying to know that at the grass-roots there are clubs where traditional values and attitudes do not bend in the wind of change.

**'We are a jolly football team, all players true and bold,
We are the Cardiff RFC whose history we'll unfold,
We cherish one ambition, its good name to maintain
And woe betide the son-of-a-gun who slights the Cardiff name'**

First verse of club song composed by D.E. 'Danny' Davies, former captain of Cardiff and president of WRU 1961-62, who died in 1985.

5
CARDIFF

Any person who has been part of a club for a reasonably long time, as I have been with Cardiff, tends to have an ambivalent attitude towards that club. You find yourself loving the club for its strengths and its imperfections. Although there are those who might argue otherwise, Cardiff is no different from any other club in that it is blessed (and blighted) with the good and the bad: the industrious and the apathetic; men of vision and others Cyclopean; some unwaveringly loyal, others cynically rebellious. This is the mix of any reasonably democratic institution, and it is the clash of the various factions which makes Cardiff tick, makes it such a fascinating club, and one which has given someone like me, a student of eccentric behaviour, unremitting pleasure. What a joy (mostly) it has been to witness the jostling and juggling, the personality tug-of-war. At the end of the day, however, what matters in any rugby club is what happens on the field, and I believe what sets Cardiff apart from many clubs is that they are not distracted from their prime purpose: to provide players with an opportunity to play. Although it was not obviously so when I first joined in 1974, Cardiff is a *players'* club, and the destiny of the club is decided by those who wear the blue and black hooped jersey week-in week-out.

The pleasure of playing for a club like Cardiff is not without its defects or its pressures. One of the problems is that you have so much to live up to. Expectation in performance is inevitably high, for you are not simply playing for yourself, for your own enjoyment, you are keenly aware of traditions also, and of the pleasure you must try to give others, particularly the supporters. This can present a dilemma to players who cannot reconcile the two philosophies: that the game is for players (ergo to hell with those who watch) or that you have to play in a particular way to satisfy those who by paying to watch make the club viable. Thank goodness the Cardiff fans, though knowledgeable and critical, are a good-natured bunch. They tolerate it when you have an off-day and generally forgive you provided you don't make a habit of it.

When I was a boy there was only one club in the world. Without being conscious of the fact, I was groomed and destined to play for Llanelli, and I had set my heart on it. At that time Cardiff was to me just another club, vague and unidentified, lying 'over there', towards the east of Tumble and Llanelli. The Scarlets, on the other hand, were the immortals and Stradey Park was redolent of the most heroic deeds and matches in Welsh rugby history. Although I had played five times for Welsh Secondary Schools, my fate as a future Llanelli player was not determined until I played for Carmarthenshire, first against North Wales at Carmarthen, and then against Monmouthshire in the Welsh County final at Stradey in April 1974. Monmouthshire had a very good side at the time, including Allan Lewis and Keith James at half-back, but a 17-year-old upstart upset all the predictions with two tries, a dropped goal and a penalty. I've always considered that one of my best matches in that everything seemed to go perfectly. Within six months I was wearing the much-prized Scarlet jersey. The biggest event of my life up to then had been against Carmarthen Athletic: my two penalty goals which won the match, putting the icing on the cake. Helen and her parents, Luther and Hilary, came to watch that first match for Llanelli, and I don't know which of the four of us was the more thrilled that I had at last become a Scarlet, albeit in a modest opener. Although Phil Bennett was the first and obvious choice, I was more than happy to play whenever Llanelli wanted me to, and apart from being on replacement duty against Tonga, I played for the Scarlets in four other matches, against Abertillery, Moseley, Orrell and Aberavon. By now I had moved east, to take up my studies at UWIST in Cardiff, and although the travelling to and from Llanelli was obviously going to cause me some problems – car-less, see – I had become accustomed to the idea of being established as Benny's deputy. Then, out of the blue, my life was completely changed by a telephone call. It was from Barry John. I was dumbfounded. 'Why don't you come down to the Arms Park and join Cardiff?' B.J. suggested, pointing out that the Cardiff fly-half position was fluid, and that life would be that much easier without having to hike all the way to Llanelli twice or three times a week. To a relatively impoverished student, for whom time and money were critical, what B.J. said made sense, and before I realised just how important the decision was, I had joined Cardiff, even though it was a big wrench to leave Stradey. Accordingly I made my debut for the blue and blacks a few weeks after my 18th birthday, against Penarth on 13 November, and I couldn't believe how lucky I was. It was even more incredible, when watching *Sports Line-up* on television a few days later, that I learned that I'd been selected to play for Cardiff *against* Llanelli the following week. The game of my life – it was almost too much to take in. I don't know how I coped, how I contained the marvellous feeling of elation. Then the bombshell burst. Llanelli refused to grant me a permit to play for Cardiff. I was shattered, numbed by what appeared to be a piddling and pointless gesture. It seemed absurd that Llanelli, with such a superb player as Benny on their books, should be that interested in a youngster still wet behind the ears. It was my first experience of the intrigues, the petty politics, of the game, and a salutary lesson, and had anyone asked me at the time I would have found it very difficult to forgive Llanelli. So Keith James played outside Gareth Edwards instead of me, and played very well in a Cardiff victory over the Scarlets, which appeared to me a fitting riposte.

Cardiff meanwhile assured me that the permit would eventually arrive and, as I was content to be part of the Cardiff set-up and play understudy to Keith, I wasn't that distressed that my rugby was for the Second XV, 'The Rags'. A month later, Cardiff picked me as travelling reserve for a Welsh Cup match, away at Ystradgynlais. I made my own way to the little village club ground, up the valley from Swansea. I had already changed by the time the team turned up. Imagine my feelings when I was told to change back again: 'Llanelli still haven't given you clearance'. As I did so, the tears streamed down my face. A couple of hard-bitten Cardiff committee men could not disguise their embarrassment at the incident.

Ultimately Llanelli relented and granted my permit, and I duly played my first 'official' match for Cardiff in the traditional Boxing Day fixture against Pontypridd. I have never discovered who at Llanelli was behind the delaying tactics, nor am I that interested now. But a clue to the thinking at Stradey lay in a statement made at the time by Handel Greville, one of their officials, to my step-brother, Mel: 'He'll learn more sitting in the stand at Stradey than he'll learn playing at Cardiff'. I wonder what he *really* meant?

The unsavoury Llanelli incident over, I began the settling-in process at Cardiff. By the end of that first season I had played 21 matches, and had recovered from the trauma of finding myself in the company of some of the great players of Welsh rugby. At the time we had a big, experienced pack and there I was, a kid of 18, with Gareth Edwards inside me and Gerald Davies outside. If I didn't learn anything from playing alongside players of that calibre, I'd never learn anything, but I don't expect Handel Greville would have appreciated that. Off the field, I was made to feel very welcome by the Cardiff officials, and I much appreciated the learned counsel and affability of Howard Norris, Keith Rowlands and John Davies in particular.

I became especially friendly with Brynmor Williams, already a Cardiff stalwart for he had joined the club two seasons previously. Being able to speak in Welsh to Brynmor was a bonus. Brynmor, however, can be blamed for leading me astray, for many was the time I followed him like a lamb for late night sessions in wine bars and the like. Apart from the fact that Brynmor was a very fine player, he had other qualities, one of which was his extensive repertoire of excuses. If you were ever stumped for a reason to get out of something, the solution would be to phone Brynmor. He should have written a book on excuses. Although we have gone our separate ways, in a rugby sense, Brynmor and I have stayed close friends. He follows me to the wine bars now.

Like all players, Brynmor was not without his critics. There were those who had never thrown a scrum-half pass in their lives, who knocked him for his capricious deliveries to his fly-half. It's not out of friendship that I reject the disparagement. The difference between a good scrum-half and a great one, in terms of passing, is consistency and whenever I played outside Brynmor that consistency was the equal of that of any other scrum-half I've played with. No scrum-half can get it right every time, but it was amusing to read of Brynmor's 'dreadful' passes which ballooned, squirted or skimmed across the grass. All I can say is that, as the man who had to take them, I was rarely disconcerted. In fact, we actually worked out a ploy to make use of one of his so-called 'bad' passes. Deliberately, he would throw the ball along the ground, well past me. This enabled me to scurry after the ball and, because at pick-up I was much wider of the defence than normal, I found myself with a lot more space and options than I would have had had I been presented with a conventional pass. We only used the 'skimmer' as an option, but it worked extremely well, and I don't think any defence realised what we were doing. Reading the newspapers the next day proved they were not alone.

There can't be that many fly-halves who have had the good fortune I had to play with as many as three brilliant scrum-halves at one club: Gareth Edwards, Brynmor and Terry Holmes. If Brynmor was unlucky it was in that he was a contemporary of Gareth and Terry, but when he did play for Cardiff I was not alone in appreciating his talents. All three were so individual, so different, that it is impossible to compare them. I would hesitate to nominate any one of them as the 'greatest' simply because that would be invidious, and I don't make that sort of judgement anyway. When I joined Cardiff, Gareth was in the superstar category, and I suppose an 18-year-old straight out of school was entitled to be over-awed. With Gareth, you certainly knew your place in the pecking order. I was given evidence of this in a Cardiff versus Llanelli match. We faced a fierce wind in the first half and Gareth threw the ball to me every time, leaving me to cope with the gale and to try to find touch. In the second half the wind was in our favour, and when we were awarded a penalty 70 yards out, I snatched up the ball confident that I'd be expected to continue doing all the kicking. G.O.E. ran up and grabbed the ball from me. 'I'll take it, young man', he declared. At the time, I was sensitive enough to feel put out by Gareth's action, and considered it somewhat selfish in view of the role allocated to me in the first half. On reflection, maybe I over-reacted.

One of the real characters from my early years at Cardiff has been Alan Phillips. Alan could be quite incorrigible, and it may be surprising that two completely contrasting people should have become friendly. I was shy to the point of diffidence, while Alan was ebullient and outspoken. It was possibly his forthrightness that cost him his place in the Welsh team, for it certainly couldn't have been his rugby. Not only is Alan a tremendous snatcher of tries – he's always high up in the list of Cardiff try-scorers – but he is an excellent support player in the loose, instinctive and very, very quick for a forward. I'd wager a few pints of Brain's that he'd out-hook any hooker at international level.

Over the years, I earned a reputation for not being the most dedicated tackler in the business, a 'fingertip tackler' as Barry John would say. Phillips helped propagate the myth. According to him, I didn't go for the ankles, I went for the throat. This came about after a Cup match against Wrexham, who had a little terrier of a scrum-half. Cheeky, too, he tried to cut inside me and I was left flat-footed. The only trouble was I left my arm out instinctively, and the Wrexham lad went down as if I'd hit him with a sledgehammer. Phillips saw the incident and immediately raced up to the referee. 'Terrible, ref', he said, pointing towards me, 'You'll have to send him off.' The rest of the lads collapsed in laughter. I would have hit Phillips with a sledgehammer if I'd had one handy.

I'm glad Alan was nominated captain of Cardiff for 1985-86. Being the character he is, he wasn't everyone's idea of a skipper. But he deserved the job. He's put in 13 years of loyal service to the club, has regularly played 30 to 40 matches a season, and he has scored a lot of tries. It'll be interesting to see what sort of job he makes of it. What is in his favour is that the present players have more or less grown up together in the club, as a team. Only a couple of players have put in less than seven to eight years service. The spirit there is tremendous. I'm sure this has been a factor in the success the club has had over the past four years. We meet, we train, we play and afterwards we enjoy, which is what being part of a rugby club is all about. On Saturday night it's ten pints of Brain's Dark and we all end up in paradise. (Well, to be more precise, the Paradise Curry House.) Rugby players are creatures of habit, it seems.

Today's set-up at Cardiff contrasts sharply with that of the old days. When I joined, team spirit was conspicuous by its absence, a consequence I suppose of the self-interest (and self-preservation) of the factions on the playing side. The team in those days was comprised of easily identifiable groups. These were the 'Glue Gang', the Guinness drinkers and the older players like Roger Lane, Gerry Wallace, P.L. Jones and Barry Nelmes; the 'Stars', Gareth Edwards, Gerald Davies and Alex Finlayson; and the 'Kids', Terry Holmes, Brynmor Williams, Mike Murphy and myself. The interaction between the various groups was absorbing, kindled on one side by a certain amount of envy and on the other by indifference, or in some cases sheer fright. All the youngsters were petrified for instance by away matches, of what the 'Glue Gang' might do to us on the coach journey. I'm not averse to a little bit of horseplay, or a bit of fun. Sometimes, however, things would get out of hand, and there was a time when I seriously contemplated opting out of playing in away matches. Once, coming back from Scotland, I became the 'victim' of a distasteful prank by Ian Robinson, who had some advantages in height and weight over me. With more of a show of bravado than any serious hope of restraining Robbo, I lunged out at him. At that very moment the coach took a sharp bend in the road, which resulted in Robbo losing his balance, cracking his head on the luggage rack and suffering a nasty gash. There was blood everywhere and pandemonium on the coach. Robbo seemed to take it all in his stride, but he did not join in the general amusement as our somewhat inebriated physio, Keith Harse, tried to stitch him up as the coach lurched homewards. Eventually, common sense prevailed, and the driver pulled into a lay-by so that the stitching could be done properly. The 'Glue Gang' ultimately went too far. Another source of their fun was to pour after-shave on some unfortunate's bare backside and then set it alight. When one player suffered third degree burns from this piece of sheer stupidity, a halt had to be called. Gerald Davies, bless him, took it upon himself to end it. As captain, Gerald had his priorities right, and although probably he lost a degree of popularity with the oldies, he was admired by the youngsters. His firmness did more than restrain the inanity, it set Cardiff on course to become a happy and successful club. We have built on Gerald's example and inspiration, and I'm sure that is reflected in our success on the field. We still have our fun, but it is harmless and doesn't (usually) offend anyone. Respect for each other is a prime factor in this.

It is interesting that Roger Beard, Cardiff's present coach, used to be a member of the 'Glue Gang'. He had to overcome some understandable prejudice from the committee, and the players to some extent, before he was fully accepted in his new role. In a club like Cardiff in which players' views are freely given and often sought, the job of coach is not easily defined. But Roger has fitted in very well. His commitment, his frankness and candour are appreciated. He also has that quality unusual in coaches – the ability to get the best out of players. Some of this I'm sure can be traced back to his association with his predecessor. The qualities of John 'Buck' Ryan have clearly rubbed off on Roger.

Buck coached Cardiff for three seasons, the first of which coincided with my year of captaincy. When he first came, he struck me as apprehensive, uncertain as to how he should deal with the players. I'm sure he thought that Holmes and Davies, for example, would be prima donnas, and that he would have his work cut out to get us to train. He was agreeably surprised by our attitude, for if nothing else Terry and I were diligent and regular attenders at Buck's sessions. Buck was a fitness fanatic. We soon discovered the meaning of the pain barrier.

Buck took almost paternal pride in the side's performance, and he was savage in his criticism if we let ourselves down. This was certainly so on our tour of South Africa in 1979. We had done very well until the penultimate match, against a Natal Country XV at Newcastle. It should have been the easiest match of the tour, but we threw it away. We thought Buck had caught rabies. He was so furious, he was almost frightening. We soon discovered that his bite was just as nasty as his bark. After the match we had a seven-hour drive, arriving in Durban at 3 am. No reasonable lie-in for us, Buck ordered. He insisted that we were up and ready to train at 8.30 am, and despite the moans and the grumbles, we were. The next two and half hours were purgatory. It was the toughest, most gruelling training session I've ever endured. All this two days before the hardest match of the tour, against Natal, who had prepared for the match with the same thoroughness as they did before playing the Lions. We won 23-15, and we played superbly. We were terrified of losing. It just shows what pure fright can do. Our best try covered 60 yards and it was a real corker, scored by Huw Davies, playing on the wing. Everybody agreed that that was Huw's finest match for Cardiff.

From then on Buck proceeded to rebuild the Cardiff side, introducing his own thinking to influence the players' attitude. There was no namby pamby nonsense from him about an expansive approach being the most important element in our game. Winning was the priority, and he reminded us of it often. Allowing for my somewhat prejudiced view of coaches and coaching, I feel confident that Buck or Roger would do an excellent job at national level, for they know how to communicate, to address themselves to players' ideas and problems.

Another facet of the Cardiff club, too often denigrated by players, is the quality of our alickadoos. We've had many tremendous characters, like Howard Norris, Dai Hayward, Peter Nyhan and Stan Bowes. Stan is the most extrovert of the

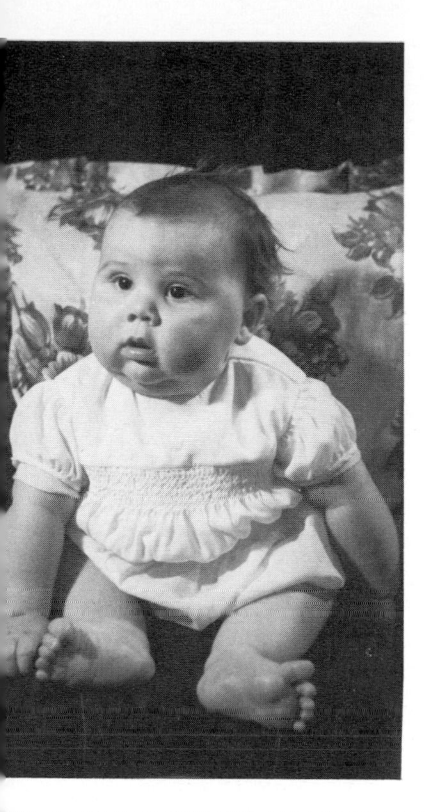

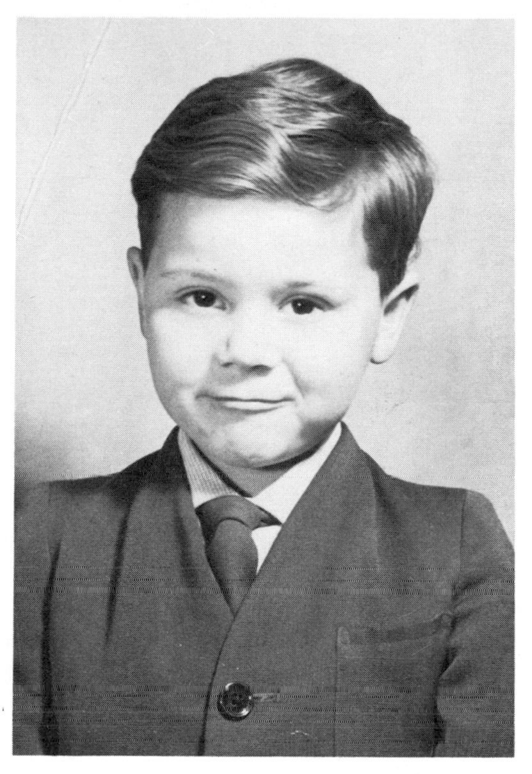

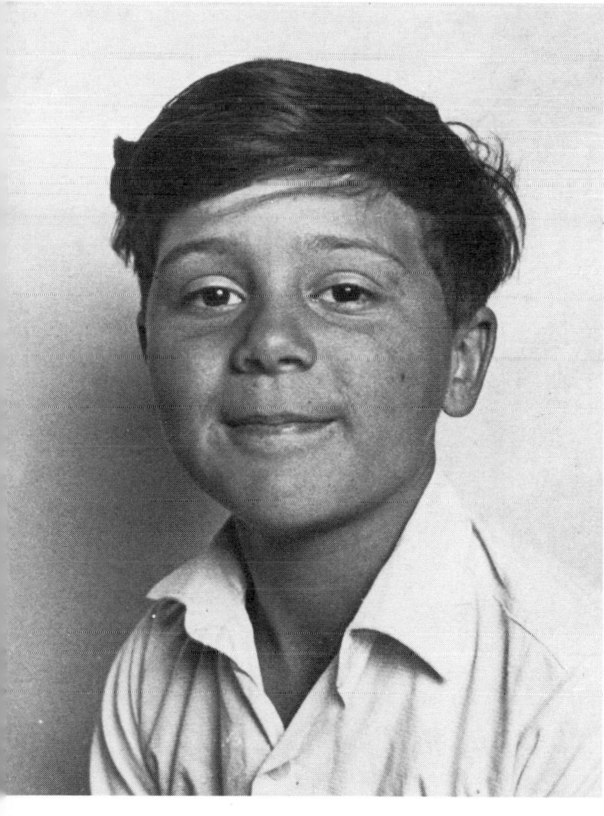

The family photo album revisited – my early days at Tumble. At six months old; as a five-year-old posing for my first school photograph at Tumble Primary School; and three years later, hot and perspiring, after some kicking practice on the school rugby pitch.

Top: Cardiff changing-rooms in 1978, shortly after Terry Holmes and I learned we had been selected to play for Wales against the All Blacks. We had more hair in those days.

Above: Terry Holmes (left), Bob Newman, Chris Webber and Neil Hutchings lend moral suppo
as I try to kick Cardiff into a good position at the Arms Park. *Western Mail and Echo*

: A birthday treat for young Matthew De Maid, son of a local solicitor. Matthew paid a visit to
Cardiff changing-rooms after we played Swansea in 1979, with Tom Holley (left), the club
siotherapist. Andrew Yeandle and Barry Nelmes (right) helped make Matthew's day.
vn White

ve: After a work-out at the Arms Park, shortly before Cardiff played New Zealand in 1980.
team was (back row) David Burcher, Ian Eidman, Jeff Whitefoot, Tony Mogridge, Robert
ster, Rhodri Lewis, Terry Holmes, Mike Watkins, W.G.D., (front row) Pat Daniels, Paul Elliott,
ı Davies, John Scott, Owen Golding and Derek Preece. *Western Mail and Echo*

Top: Helen and I after our wedding on 5 May 1979, at St John's Church, Pontyberem, with De
Quinnell (left), Jeff Squire and Terry Holmes, all members of the Wales Triple Crown side th
year, keeping team spirit alive.

Above: Just like Dad. Kathryn, four months old, is obviously not amused. *Elwyn White*

ɔove: Kathryn enjoying her
st Christmas, 1982, with
am Tumble' and 'Dad
ımble' showing suitable
andparental interest.

ght: One of my favourite
otographs of Kathryn, aged
months, May 1983.

Top: My Cardiff colleague John Scott giving instructions to the photographer in the week befor
we were on opposite sides, Wales versus England in 1981. Scottie didn't stop rabbiting in the
match, but to no avail. Wales won 21-19, a nice start for Brynmor Williams' international caree
News of the World/Bob Thomas

Above: Steve Fenwick moves in to support as I'm collared by John Rutherford in the Scotland
versus Wales match on 7 February 1981 at Murrayfield. Steve and I remember the date well.
was his last appearance in a Welsh jersey, and I was dropped, too, after Scotland won 15-6. T
other players showing interest in events are 'Ikey' Stephens, Bob Ackerman, Rhodri Lewis an
Dai Richards. *Colorsport*

les against France on 6 February 1982. Not one of my most memorable kicks. The day
onged to Gwyn Evans, whose six penalty goals equalled the world record shared by Don
rke (New Zealand) and Gerald Bosch (South Africa). *Colorsport*

Above: Want to bet this pass was intercepted too? Jim Calder brings me down, Colin Deans follows up and (right) Roger Baird waits for unconsidered trifles in an example of the action from Wales' disaster day against Scotland, 20 March 1982. Scotland scored 34 points, the highest total by any side in Wales, which was no doubt a factor in my being cast out into the international wilderness for three years. *Colorsport*

Right: My final home appearance for Wales, against Ireland at the Arms Park on 16 March 1985. Ireland won 21-9, their first win at Cardiff for 18 years. Note the intriguing angle of Bob Ackerman's run, which seems inadvertently to block out Mike Kiernan. *Colorsport*

lot, and he is supreme when conducting the committee choir, or gleefully and loudly maligning 'them black and amber bastards' from Newport, or the 'bloody Jacks' from Swansea. Stan's rendering of 'Tiger Bay', the 'Kardiff Nashnul Anthem', has to be heard to be believed. Real 'Kardiff', is Stan, and proud of it.

Bowesy was elected chairman in 1984-85, and the players were surprised that he also found time to manage our tour to Thailand. Gary Davies went as assistant manager and between them they smoothed our path through that fascinating country. Bowesy obviously had great faith in Gary, and whenever he wanted advice or support, a raucous 'Gary! Gary! Gary!' became a familiar cry throughout the tour. One night after over-indulging in local hospitality, Stan called plaintively for Gary. 'Where the hell is he?' demanded Stan. Gary was standing four yards away. So that's what they mean by blind drunk.

There is no harder working member of the committee than Peter Nyhan, although he has had a chequered past. He's probably the only committee man ever to have been suspended. He had his knuckles rapped over an incident with Alan Phillips in a pub in Usk, after being in charge of an away trip. It says much for Peter that he holds no grudges, and returned to the fold after his suspension. A lot of so-called loyal club men would never have deigned to darken our doors again if it had happened to them.

Everyone, of course, has their favourite people at a club. Among mine are Nancy and Ted John, honorary proprietors of the club shop, which is a grand name for the Portakabin at the entrance to the clubhouse. Ever cheerful and good-natured, nothing is too much trouble for Nancy and Ted. They go out of their way to make all feel welcome at Cardiff, friend and stranger alike. They also do a good job in a practical sense, because the shop's profits are an important part of the club's income. In September 1985 Ted heard that this book was shortly to be published. 'The shop'll have a couple of hundred copies', promised Ted, a few moments before I ran out on to the field against Neath. That was the best thing I did all afternoon. I had a stinker. Ted obviously thought so too. After the match he came up to me, his eyes full of censure, and said: 'You can forget that order for the book'. It was his joking way of commenting on my performance – at least I hope he was joking. Anyway, Nancy and Ted have got a friend for life in my daughter Kathryn. After Cardiff beat Australia in 1984, they gave her a huge blue and black Teddy Bear, which she absolutely adores. I wonder if it was their way of saying they thought I had a good game?

In an age when rugby football has expanded worldwide, and fixtures inevitably take on a much more cosmopolitan appearance, there is still much to be said for maintaining traditional links with clubs, of continuing associations that go back into the distant past.

One of Cardiff's oldest fixtures is against Moseley, who were first met on 11 November 1880. Generally speaking, Cardiff have had the better of the English club since then, but the special toe-hold Moseley have in Cardiff's history does not concern any of our many victories over them, but a defeat, which occurred at the Arms Park on 17 April 1886 by two goals to a try (10-3). It was the last match of the season for Frank Hancock's celebrated side, and for them to lose at the final hurdle was particularly galling, for until then they had won every match in one of the most extraordinary seasons ever. Cardiff had won comfortably at Moseley earlier in the season and, incredibly, by the time they came to the last match, only two sides, Moseley and Gloucester, had scored against them, and another, Swansea, were beaten four times. Moseley's victory not only ruined what would have been our best-ever season but embarrassed preparations for the suitable celebration of a 100 per cent record.

Subsequent Cardiff captains have often been reminded of that blot in our record book, and the beating of Moseley understandably is given some priority. There are times, however, when the team can be positively amnesic about past insults. It is then the job of the captain to whip up flagging interest with passion and oratory. I couldn't be one of those captains who'd let the club down, could I? Was I one to duck my responsibilities? Definitely not. Now passion and oratory are not exactly my speciality, but duty is duty, and so at The Reddings in 1980 I launched into my pre-match tirade, my team-talk. History, pride and duty were the chief ingredients of that dressing-room sermon. At first, the boys listened attentively but amazement at the performance soon gave way to tittering. Exasperated by their obvious lack of concern, I became desperate. 'If you don't pull your fingers out, we'll go down that M6 with our legs between our tails', I implored. At least, that's what they told me I said. I'm a little vague about it. I couldn't hear myself think with all the laughter and hoots of derision. Regardless, I trust the anecdote demonstrates that we serious-minded players do have a keener sense of history than might be imagined.

There are those, I suppose, who might dispute Cardiff's claim to be the greatest club in the world. Personally, I don't think there is any room for debate. The achievements are in the record book, and must stand favourable comparison with those of any other club, if the criterion is to have beaten every major side at one time or another. It would be hard to imagine, either, any club coming remotely close to Cardiff's ratio of victories to defeats. If other evidence is required, surely nothing can compare with the club's unparalleled list of international players, a total boosted in one remarkable period when Cardiff supplied 98 players out of the 195 chosen by Wales in 13 internationals between 1946 and 1949. Not bad Cardiff, not bad at all.

'Skill comes so slow, and life so fast doth fly,
We learn so little and forget so much'

Sir John Davies

6
FROM UWIST TO OXFORD

One of the most enjoyable periods of my life without qualification was my three years at the University of Wales Institute of Science and Technology, better known by its acronym UWIST, which is not only easier to say but is, I understand, a godsend to writers of headlines in newspapers.

UWIST is a big, rambling collection of buildings in the centre of Cardiff and when as a shy little lad from the country I first went there (in 1974) I was awe-struck by its size, and the number of students and staff scurrying this way and that for all the world like ants around an ant-hill. Yet before I realised what was happening I was part of it, swallowed up in the turmoil of the place. After the relative tranquillity and the slow measured pace of Gwendraeth Grammar and Tumble, UWIST, and the frenetic way of life in a city, were a shock to the system. Nevertheless, I was amazed how easy the transition was. I didn't start singing 'the city life for me', but I found I liked what I saw, and eventually I came to love being part of it.

I was fortunate that on my first day at UWIST I fell in with three lads from the Rhondda. Howard Jeffrey, Dai Gregson and Rob Middleton were real characters, and we became the closest of friends during our three years in Cardiff. All of us played rugby, for one or other of the three XVs run at UWIST on Wednesdays, and regardless of our respective success on the field we became like the Four Musketeers socially – all for one and one for all. Evenings were a grub crawl as much as a pub crawl. It was down to the Old Arcade, then on to Monty's or Qui Qui's before we arrived at our final destination, El Grec's in Caroline Street. After a life of plain honest eating at home, I don't know how my stomach coped with the ale and often exotic food. It was no wonder that I went down with peritonitis in my third year at UWIST.

It is said that university life is character-building. I don't know about that, but UWIST certainly changed me. When I went there I must have seemed a classic mummy's little boy, away from home for the first time. Shy, reserved, insecure, I stood out like the metaphoric sore thumb. I graduated in more senses than one at UWIST, for it was there that I learned the importance of self-reliance, of confidence in myself. In other words I grew up. This made a big difference, I believe, to my rugby career, for my first year at UWIST coincided with my introduction to the first-class game. I played for Llanelli, then Cardiff, and in my second year I toured Canada with the Barbarians and became a Welsh sub. Somehow, I found time for study too, and the fact that I managed a BSc (Hons) in Applied Science gave me a sense of achievement academically. Quite why I chose to read Science I don't know, except perhaps that at school I enjoyed chemistry and thought I'd give it a whirl.

The first year at UWIST was probably the most memorable, because everything was new and challenging. I lived in the Hall of Residence, Traherne Hall in Penylan, which meant a short, sharp walk into Cardiff for lectures. It was at that time that I began to acquaint myself with Cardiff and came to realise what a fascinating place it is – lovely, but often unappreciated. It is extraordinary the number of visitors to the city who never take the trouble to look around. Some think of Cardiff as the walk from the railway station to the Arms Park and back again, the instant tour. No wonder prejudice about Cardiff is so rife. In fact it is a marvellous place, full of character and contrasts, with history at almost every turn and many fine buildings apart from the Civic Centre which far more august observers than I have declared to be among the finest of any city. The Docks, Tiger Bay, as it was, Canton, and Cathay's all have a flavour and fascination of their own. In the words of the old Cardiff song: 'if you haven't been down Tiger Bay, you haven't seen Cardiff at all'.

At Traherne Hall I roomed with Roger Jones, an old pal from Gwendraeth and my team-mate and scrum-half at school. Roger, a cousin of Barry John's, must have found me tolerable company for we then shared a bedsit together in Cathay's for two years. Tolerable might not be the precise word. After a few ales, I had a habit of sleepwalking. Many was the time Roger would wake in the early hours to find me opening a wardrobe, putting on my jeans, or doing other odd things. Roger was a very good player, and had he persevered I'm sure he'd have got to the top, or at least have gained some recognition. In his three years at UWIST Roger never spent one weekend in Cardiff. He was back home to Cefneithin as regular as clockwork. He was the epitome of a Welsh lad, a genuine home-lover. Those that criticise the Welsh as, for instance, bad tourists, probably have failed to recognise our 'weakness' in being so attached to our homes. It is part of our nature.

That bedsit at 12 Llandough Street, Cathay's, was a real home from home for both of us. Mrs Rees was not your archetypal landlady. By odd coincidence she was from Tumble, but had lived in Cardiff for over 20 years. A widow, the kindly Mrs Rees generally acted as a second mother to me. For the two years I was in her care, as it were, she charged me four pounds a week, which included Sunday lunch. She also laundered my rugby kit. I had shamefacedly tried to hide the muddied heap behind my bedroom curtains, and I couldn't believe my eyes when I returned to find it beautifully washed and ironed. That wasn't part of our contract, but it became a tacit agreement that I'd continue hiding the gear and she'd find it and launder it. A wonderful lady, Mrs Rees.

Another person with a benevolent attitude towards me was UWIST's registrar, Frank Harris-Jones, a Cambridge graduate from Merthyr. I found the period of exams at the end of the first year very stressful, and Frank recognised my panic. He took me under his wing and talked me through the exams. The following year (1975) he came to the rescue again. I'd been invited to tour Canada with the Baa-Baas, a fantastic opportunity at the time, but the tour coincided with further exams. Frank's persuasive qualities were brought into play once more, and he managed to talk my Dean of Faculty into allowing me to go and to set special papers for me to take a month after my return. Frank even allowed me the use of his flat to work for those exams while he was on holiday. His indulgence meant a lot – without it I'd never have gone to Canada, that's for sure. We've kept in touch since those days, and we occasionally get out for meals together. Usually the talk is of rugby – he has become a Cardiff supporter. Naturally I have reciprocated. I have become a fan of the theatre, specifically Stratford where I've gone with him to watch another of his friends, Judi Dench. We're never far from rugby, though. Judi's husband, Mike Williams, is a bit of a fan, too.

While at UWIST, during that first year, I also got to know Carwyn James comparatively well. As luck would have it, he occupied a house next door to Traherne Hall, although I did not realise it at the time. One day a few of us were playing football on a grassy space opposite Carwyn's house when he came over, obviously recognising me. After a bit of chat, he asked us whether we'd like to accompany him to Rodney Parade to watch Newport play Bristol. We felt flattered by his interest. Roger, myself and Dave Smyth (UWIST's captain who later skippered Ballymena and Ulster) went along, finding ourselves in the Press box as our famous rugby writer made notes for his report for the *Guardian.* I don't know whether his expenses stretched that far, but Carwyn then treated us to fish and chips in Newport before inviting us back to his house for a nightcap. What a nightcap! Out came Carwyn's favourite tipple, gin, and this he dispensed liberally as we talked rugby non-stop until well past the hour that little boys like us should have been abed. I've never seen Carwyn more relaxed, and it was fascinating, as well as a privilege, to listen to his views on rugby generally. If anyone ever loved a sport, it was Carwyn, and there can have been few who could address themselves to the game with such clarity and originality. I realise that others have expressed their dismay that Welsh rugby refused to employ his genius, but when one looks at the impoverished state of our game today, it seems totally illogical that such talent went unrealised in his own country. Had he been given the helm, had he set the coaching policy, what rich legacy would he have left us, how different might the game we have be now?

My rugby at UWIST can be summed up in three words: fun, success and near-disaster. The fun came mainly in my first year. The success was in the second, 1975. I ended up in hospital in the third.

No-one took us very seriously in 1974, in a rugby sense, but everyone sat up and took notice the following season when UWIST won the UAU title, the chief prize for red-brick universities. I have to say immediately that Swansea University, our opponents in the final at Twickenham, were victims of daylight robbery. It would be fair to say that we were outplayed in most aspects of the match, and that Swansea were far better value than their 4-3 lead suggested, our penalty being scored by our rather short-sighted wing, Richard Williams, who rammed one over from 55 yards. With a minute to go, Swansea looked certain to hold out. For us to win, some heroics were required, something desperate needed to be done. I drew the short straw. From the only line-out we won in the match, I pumped up a high Garryowen to Ken Hopkins, Swansea's full-back, the safest pair of hands on the field. Not this time. Ken must have panicked and a real bumble fumble 30 yards out gave us the scrum. We'd had difficulty winning our scrum ball, but we won this, the most crucial of all. Mick Connors (who later joined Wasps) was so keen to get the ball to me quickly that he threw an entirely forgettable pass, a real daisy-cutter. Instinctively I made a grab for it as it reached my toes, the ball stuck, and I let fly a drop-kick with blind haste, hope and a prayer. It could have gone anywhere, but instead it sailed smack through the middle. It was over! Incredibly, unbelievably, we had won. 'The sweetest kick ever to have left a Welshman's foot' said the *Guardian*. Little did that writer know. The match will ever remain my favourite. I'm told the team plus 100-odd supporters had a magnificent night out in London. I can't comment. I believe they call it alcoholic amnesia. A couple of years later, I was reunited with two of the luckless Swansea players, Ken Hopkins and Byron Light. We went up to Oxford together.

The following year (1976) we reached the semi-final, and everybody at UWIST had high hopes that we would get to Twickenham again. But for me it was a time of pain and hospital. A week before the semi-final I went down with peritonitis, and I was whisked away for surgery. After the operation, Glan Jones, UWIST's Sports Administrator, our Mr Fixit and a real Arthur Daley, came visiting. The success of the operation had been touch and go, apparently, and I was not feeling that marvellous as I lay in bed, with tubes protruding everywhere. Glan's first words were: 'Thank you for letting us down next week'. Helen, who was at my bedside, nearly floored him. I don't think she appreciated Glan's attempt at a joke to cheer me up. I was still in hospital when I heard that UWIST had lost the semi-final. The final epitaph on the operation: I also missed Cardiff's Welsh Cup final against Newport. Cardiff went to Canada without me as well, because of my final exams. My three years at UWIST thus ended on a pretty dismal note. But if things looked black one moment, the next they had brightened up considerably and I was soon preparing for another challenge, a post-graduate course at Oxford University. I took my boots, of course, just in case.

I don't think even in my wildest imaginings – and I've had some of those – I would ever have considered going to Oxford. I was sold the idea at a Cardiff centenary dinner late in 1976 during conversation with Carwyn James and Onllwyn Brace. It's strange how big events often follow small chat. 'What do you intend doing when you leave UWIST?' inquired Carwyn. 'I have no plans, really', I replied cautiously, because I realised Carwyn was sounding me out, trying to discover whether I'd be returning home to play for Llanelli. Onllwyn interceded. 'Why don't you go up to Oxford for a year?' he suggested. 'You'll have a wonderful time and it could do you some good. It'll be an experience.' Onllwyn was not exactly scouting, but as a former Oxford player he felt obliged to try whenever he could to encourage experienced players to 'go up' to bolster Dark Blue fortunes, which were at that time at their lowest ever after five Cambridge wins on the trot. I didn't worry one jot about Onllwyn's motives. As I had no practical immediate plans, it seemed a marvellous idea. I'd love to go, I told him. Suffice it to say, Onllwyn knew just the right people to talk to, and before I knew it I was Oxford bound, seeking a Diploma of Education and, with luck, a Blue. Luck, as it happened, played a big part in my short stay at Britain's oldest university.

A Dip. Ed. year at Oxford is in reality only eight months, and if you are keen and part of the rugby set-up it is a hectic, feverish period, when time flashes by and you finish up wishing you had done many other things. My enjoyment of Oxford life was diluted by a nagging leg injury, although I never allowed my enthusiasm to waver. Like a sponge, I soaked up Oxford; its history, its traditions, the remarkable architecture. No dull and witless city, Oxford. University life there was different inevitably in many ways from UWIST, and it took me some time to adjust to the more formal atmosphere. Some Oxford habits I found a challenge to my home-spun sense of values, but it was never dull, and my perception I'm sure was sharpened by different disciplines and attitudes. I grew up at UWIST. I matured at Oxford. Friends made the going easy. As I've said, my experience was shared by Ken Hopkins and Byron Light, and we three easy-going Welshmen artlessly found ourselves in interesting encounters with some fellow students. Very confident, we found, some ex-public schoolboys. In the early days, we were often the butt of their jokes, and we could have come from Outer Mongolia for all they knew about our background. As we became established, and accepted, the roles were reversed. Our humour and leg-pulling held the stage. We Welsh are not as daft as we look, mun.

As post-graduates, there was no college accommodation for us, so we began a search for suitable premises. The only thing available seemed to be Bed & Breakfast, Out By 7.30 am, In By 10 pm, which held little appeal for three rugby lads. Eventually, I had a brainwave. I rang Geoff Windsor-Lewis, secretary of the Barbarians. Partner in a firm of estate agents, was Geoff, I revealed confidently to Ken and Byron. Well, Geoff came up trumps. He found a property for us which was being let for 12 months – perfect, we agreed. It turned out to be an immaculate four-bedroomed, detached house on a private estate at Farmoor, four miles from Oxford. You could see the yachts and the boats on a nearby reservoir from the upstairs windows. Duw, we thought, we've arrived. The only possible hitch, it seemed, was the interview with the owners, shortly off to Germany on a year's contract. How would they react to meeting three boozy, long-haired, uncouth rugby players? We considered the situation. We eventually agreed. Diplomacy was called for. Rugby would *not* be mentioned at the interview, as John Cleese would have said. We ran through the script. I was to be a golfer, Ken an ornithologist and Byron an academic. We walked into the house, confident but apprehensive, just like before a match at Pontypool Park. The lady of the house met us in the hallway and, in a lovely lilting Welsh accent, exclaimed: 'Why, aren't you Gareth Davies, the rugby player?' Tea, Welsh cakes, smiles all around, and we were safely in our new home.

I was nominated cook and domestic, Byron did the shopping and helped me in the kitchen and generally kept the house tidy. Ken, well he did nothing. Born lazy. Worse still, on Saturday nights after a few beers, he was a real pain – your good old-fashioned bore, a real heavy. Many a night Byron and I fled from his ramblings, usually by pinching his car and going somewhere we knew he wouldn't find us. (Years later I met Ken in South Africa several times. He'd not improved one bit. He'd graduated in his pet quirk and had become one of the world's worst bores – a Welsh exile.) Despite this, we were of course all great friends, and Ken often drove me to Wales so that I could play for Cardiff midweek. After the 'Varsity Match in 1977, in which we all played, we still shared the house, although in the meantime Ken and Byron had joined London Welsh. Inevitably we'd be facing each other when the two clubs met and so it happened, in a morning match at Old Deer Park on the day of the England versus Wales match, 4 February 1978. What are friends for but to try out your best shots on? Within two minutes I'd booted the best up-and-under of my life towards Ken. Good boy, he forgot how safe he was under a high ball, and dropped it. That was bad enough. Worse was he was simultaneously thumped by both our centres and then rolled over by our forwards. Next day, he still bought me a pint in our local at Farmoor. That was quite a day in other respects. None of us had tickets for Twickenham, so we stayed in the London Welsh clubhouse to watch the match on a big screen. The picture was a bit hazy. Somebody, I've no idea who, kept bringing us jugs of beer all afternoon.

My first term at Oxford was a mixture of high elation and morbid self-pity. I trained so hard in June and July that I attained the best fitness of my life. You rarely get a chance to become super-fit and I found the idea of being a full-time player and student very appealing. Then calamity – during the holidays I was training with Llanelli at Stradey Park when I badly wrenched a knee. I've said elsewhere that one specialist warned I might never play again. It was a terrible time for me, the most frustrating period of my life, and I owe much to the skill and patience of Dr John Williams, one of Britain's leading authorities on sports injuries. Frequent visits to Dr Williams at Farnham Park, near Slough, not only helped my physical recovery – his confidence that I'd be perfectly fit in due time was an important pyschological boost. Nevertheless it was nearly six months before I fully recovered. The injury nearly cost me my Blue.

The 'Varsity Match, or more correctly the University Match, is always played on the first Tuesday in December and as the day approached, it was obvious I was not going to be 100 per cent fit. I can't imagine any match demanding more intense preparation for, after three to four months' comparatively hard work, in the final month you are required to train every day, sometimes twice a day. If I'd been fully fit, I'm sure I'd have enjoyed every minute of it. My biggest problem concerned sprinting – I couldn't. Tim Bryan, the captain, monitored the form and fitness of all his available players and he must have been sceptical in my case for I had to construct all sorts of excuses for missing the sprint sessions which were held on the Iffley Road running track. My tutor at St Catherine's College was roped into the subterfuge, telling Tim that I had important tutorials. I knew that if Tim considered I was unfit, I wouldn't play. Miraculously, I got away with it. I was named to play against Cambridge in the 96th 'Varsity Match. Ken and Byron were also in the side, so the Taffs had plenty to celebrate.

The junketing was even more protracted after the match, because we were part of the first Oxford victory since 1971. Cambridge had won the previous five matches – a record – and therefore it was particularly satisfying to have brought their run to an end. It was a wet, spiteful day and although Oxford won by only 16-10, we outplayed them tactically. They had some good players – including Eddie Butler and John Robbie – but they didn't adapt to the conditions. We decided on ten-man rugby, and it worked, because we kept rolling them back with kicks to touch and then pinning them down. Tony Watkinson kicked four penalties and Malcolm Moir scored a try. It was a good job of work, carefully planned and well carried out. A team effort, and just reward for all the sweat and toil beforehand. The man who said winning is not that important is an ass.

The night out at the Café Royal in the West End was superb. Helen accompanied me, and as I soaked up the atmosphere, I reflected on the comparison with UWIST and those nights at El Grec's back in Cardiff. There it was Brain's Dark and/or plonk and curry, at Oxford we had port and roast chestnuts at Vincent's Club and ale at that remarkable institution, the Honesty Bar, at St Edmund Hall. No different really.

Because of the injury I'd played only one match for Oxford before the 'Varsity Match, against London Scottish. In the second term the rugby is much more relaxed, and the emphasis is on enjoying playing. Winning was not critical – such a contrast with Welsh club rugby. So my second term was mainly involved with academic work and teaching practice. That was a real eye-opener. I went to Cowley St John Comprehensive School to teach Chemistry and that experience ended all my ambitions to become a teacher. I was shocked at the attitude that prevailed at Cowley. The pupils had no interest in learning, and the narrow outlook extended to the staff-room where the bitchiness and incessant 'shop' talk left me utterly disillusioned.

I was offered the chance to stay on at Oxford and continue my studies. But the need to think about earning a living after four years as a student prevailed. Anyway Helen's patience was wearing thin, for we had more or less decided we would get married when I'd had my academic fling, as it were. We settled on the date, May 1979. It meant a reluctant goodbye to Oxford and out into the big wide world to get a job. That the decision coincided with the most marvellous 12 months of my life was happy chance. After the 'Varsity Match, really the start of that special year, I returned fully fit for Cardiff, and then found myself picked by Wales for Australia. The world seemed a wonderful place in 1978.

'What flatters a man is that you think him worth flattering'

George Bernard Shaw

7
PORTRAIT OF A PARTNERSHIP

Terence David Holmes, a product of Bishop Hannon School in Cardiff, was a member of the Cardiff RFC Youth team when he and I first played together in October 1975, for Cardiff at Pontypool. Since then we have been playing partners, in a variety of sides, on over 200 occasions, which implies not only that we have become pretty familiar with each other's play, but also that we have spent more time in each other's company than, say, some married couples do in a lifetime. Add the many hours we have been together training, travelling and socialising, and Helen and Sue, our respective wives, could easily make out a case for desertion if not grounds for divorce. Fortunately the four of us have become very close friends, and both Terry and I have made great efforts, particularly in recent years, to ensure that our wives do not become rugby widows. A candlelit dinner at a posh restaurant, after-match drinks at the club and local, and visits to each other's homes all add up to a comparatively stable and tranquil home life. The girls still may not forgive us all our trespasses – 'not *another* night out with the boys?' – but thankfully they seem to be more understanding these days. They also realise that our life in rugby is not going to go on forever, and that one day, when it is all over, they'll be shooing us out of the house and accusing us of getting under their feet (at least I hope so; you've got to get some practice in on the golf course, haven't you?).

It was only when I began totting up the number of times that Terry and I played as a half-back partnership that it occurred to me that we might have set some record or other as a pair. Certainly there can be few half back pairings which have survived nearly a decade, and have played as many matches as we have, for most of that time at a competitively high level – for Cardiff, Barbarians, Wales, British Lions and a multitude of other representative sides.

We still look back at that first match, however, and wonder at the temerity of the Cardiff selection committee in deciding to throw two lambs into the lions' den at Pontypool Park. With Gareth Edwards and Brynmor Williams unavailable, it was Terry's debut for Cardiff. To two so young and ingenuous – Terry was 18 and I was 19 – 'Pooler's' reputation meant little. For all we knew we could have been going to a tea party at the vicarage. On the way to the match, Mike Knill, one of our burly forwards, asked me casually: 'Have you played against Pontypool before?' I told him no. 'Don't worry', promised Mike sullenly, 'We'll take care of you.' My heart sank, my legs felt like jelly. What on earth did he mean?

As it happened, big Mike had no need for concern. Innocence itself has many a wile, and the youthful Cardiff half-backs ran the show. In the first five minutes I slotted a couple of dropped goals, then a couple of penalty goals, and the match was as good as over. Terry meanwhile stood up manfully to the Pontypool pack, which helped give me the confidence to control events behind. The Holmes-Davies partnership had survived its baptism. We had arrived.

I suppose by now Pontypool can't bear the sight of me. I've played against them 19 times, and I've kicked more penalties (27) and more dropped goals (13) against them than against any other Welsh side. You can love Pooler, or censure them, but you never have less than respect for them. They have a knack of bringing out the best in you.

At first Terry and I were strangers to each other. We rarely chatted, and never seriously, about the game, or anything, until 1977, a year before we were both capped. This is partly explained by our relatively different backgrounds and interests. He was Cardiff-born and Cardiff-bred, and a catholic, while I was then still a bit of an outsider, a chapel boy from Welsh-speaking West Wales who had more in common with Brynmor Williams. Terry was also working for a living, whilst I was a student, which must have struck him as a fancy-free life anyway. But if we had nothing which could bring us closely together off the field, there was certainly rapport on it, that hand-in-glove association, that telepathic partnership which bound us together, but for which there was no straightforward or logical explanation.

No half-backs become acknowledged as a pair of course without the link that unites them, the pass from one to the other. The old cliché 'You just throw it and I'll catch it' certainly applied. Terry was criticised for the slowness of his pass by everyone except the man who had to take it. No-one asked me for my comments on his passing. I'd have told them they were always just where I wanted them. When Terry occasionally went astray, a glare from me was enough to convey displeasure. That used to be the signal. Now it's a smile, not a scowl, but it's enough to ensure that the subsequent passes will be spot on. The world knows how ruggedly competitive Terry is and he is renowned for his strength. You feel he could crush a man's ribs if he was so inclined. But off the field he is a real softie, a marshmallow man, who'd prefer gently to chide someone rather than rebuke him. He's never malicious in his criticism, and if he believes in something implicitly he will defend his position with powerful and eloquent argument. Although I do not share all his views on the current Welsh squad scene, I respect and understand his position. His quiet, thoughtful disposition has given many people the wrong impression. He has an honesty and candour which are rare, and no-one could have a more loyal and trustworthy friend. He's also in his element with children. He adores them, and spends hours playing with my little girl Kathryn, and his niece Rachel and nephew Thomas. We became close, I suppose, partly because Helen and Sue also hit it off. We all met up for the first time at the Aberaeron Sevens in 1977 and since then the girls seem to spend as much time together as Terry and I do. *Quid pro quo* as Germaine Greer might say.

One of the problems of being so closely associated as a pair is that it invites attention. I remember being very angry over an article in the *South Wales Echo* which was headlined

'The Odd Couple'. Terry was depicted as a rough-and-ready Cardiffian, a Brain's Dark drinker, while I was the smoothie, the gin-and-tonic-drinking, elegantly dressed young executive. If anything the reverse was true, because by then Terry had established himself and was teaching me a few things about the world of business and finance – and drinking. The writer was trying to contrast our different backgrounds, but even then he did not get it quite right. We were not so different. Both of us came from homes in which money was tight and luxuries rare, and old-fashioned values were important. If we were odd at all, it was because we had so much in common. We had similar temperaments and generally adopted similar thinking about the game. I like to feel we are both very competitive.

When I captained Cardiff I think the job helped me to mature as a player. This has certainly been the case with Terry. He made an excellent job of captaining Cardiff in 1984-85. He did a good job for Wales, too, although he did not get much credit for it. His confidence has grown enormously as well, and he is much more relaxed, more positive, when dealing with the media.

After we were capped, we were often asked to do things as a pair. We did one particular Radio Wales programme, a ten-minute slot, but because of our amateur status we were not allowed to accept payment. The fee would have to go to the WRU or a nominated club. I asked the BBC to send my fee to Tumble RFC and Terry suggested his be forwarded to a local Cardiff club, St David's, to which he was affiliated, having been a member of Cardiff Youth. Within a month Tumble had 'reimbursed' me, to cover expenses for attending various functions. Terry was somewhat envious, for there was no similar response from his club. A little later he received a letter, expressing profuse thanks for his donation, for his kind gesture in thinking of a small club. In return they invited him to attend their annual dinner. The letter was from St David's RFC, Pembrokeshire – a hundred miles away!

One of Terry's great qualities is that nothing is too much trouble for him when it comes to helping out his mates. A good example of this occurred in 1984, when he, Albert Francis, the

Arms Park groundsman, and myself, drove to Manchester in Terry's car to collect kit from Bukta for our tour of Thailand. Also in the car was a pigeon basket and four racing birds. As a favour to a friend, Terry had promised to take the birds and release them when we arrived. Shortly after the start of our relatively important meeting with the Bukta directors in their boardroom, Terry asked to be excused. He'd only be a few moments, he said. I looked out of the boardroom window. There was Terry, in the car park, taking out the basket and releasing the birds. He had not forgotten his promise.

Both Terry and I would agree that we owe much of our success as a partnership to the many good players that we played with at Cardiff. Few half-backs can prosper without an effective pack of forwards, and although Terry is probably one of the best scrum-halves in the world because of his ability to play well behind a beaten pack, he was not required to prove it very often at Cardiff. We have been fortunate indeed in the quality of our forwards, in the tight and in the loose. Competition for places is always keen, and occasionally the most difficult problem is deciding who has to be left out. I remember feeling distinctly uncomfortable on one occasion at being the conveyor of bad news over selection. For the 1980 match against the All Blacks, Cardiff had to choose between two of the best hookers in the game, Spikey Watkins (now with Newport) and Alan Phillips, who was then the Welsh hooker. Alan, with whom I was very friendly, rang me to ask if he had been selected. I told him, sorry, Spikey had got the nod. Alan was bitterly disappointed. I wasn't very happy either that I was the one who had to tell him.

There were many other good players at Cardiff whose ability was recognised and appreciated only within the club. John Davies, from Lampeter, was a prime example. He was a highly talented full-back with hardly a flaw in his game, yet often he was dismissed as good at sevens but less so at 15-a-side. Our current full-back, Paul 'Pablo' Rees, has also been unlucky to have missed out in the high honours of the game. Pablo, like Holmesy a product of Bishop Hannon School, is a superb all-round full-back, highly competitive and with a great temperament. Less capable players have won caps for Wales. He has that enviable ability to survive a real booze-up on Friday night and still produce the goods the next afternoon. Off the field, Pablo is often the life and soul of the party, a naturally funny guy. Occasionally he has stepped out of line, and has been carpeted for it. Once during the late 1970s, after a match at Swansea, the team called in for some refreshments at Pyle RFC. Pablo took an instant liking to an attractive girl and when she left the room, presumably to visit the powder room, our love-struck hero unwisely decided to follow her. The consequences did not occur to him. He went into the ladies' loo, stretched up and peeped over the cubicle door. Sitting there, staring back at him, was the Pyle chairman's wife. She was not amused. Nor were Cardiff. Pablo found himself suspended.

Again risking a charge of nepotism, Cardiff have been fortunate to have had some excellent wings, including Adrian 'Adolf' Hadley and Gerald Cordle. Gerald works very hard at his game, always eager to add quality to his pace and determination. Adolf is in my view the best wing in Wales since Gerald Davies, a casual cavalier if ever there was one. We make sure we bring him into the action as often as possible, otherwise his concentration wavers. More often than not, he's much more interested in the possibility of spotting a blonde in the crowd.

It was inevitable that Mark Ring would end up being called 'Ringo'. Ringo's opening gambit to most people he meets is 'I was born to wear No. 10', and I'll wager he's praying for the day that I retire so that he can move from the centre to fly-half and prove his claim. In my opinion Ringo is a very good centre. He too has an extraordinary temperament. Absolutely nothing concerns him on the field. Against Aberavon in the 1984-85 season he threw the most terrible pass and Gary Matthews latched on to it and scored. With a Welsh team place on the line, most players would have hidden their heads in shame, and their game would have immediately gone to pieces. Not Ringo. As he walked back he said drily: 'I hope they cut that bit out of *Rugby Special* tonight'. The next moment he made amends, brilliantly. He slashed through Aberavon's defence with pace and deception to lay on a superb try for Alun Donovan.

Alun himself is a very good centre in his own right. Ringo tends to grab the headlines, but Alun's quiet, unassertive authority has added another dimension to Cardiff's back division. Alun is a much underrated player, and has contributed greatly to our recent success. It seems incredible that Swansea picked Tony Swift in the centre for the 1983 Cup final and left Alun occupying a bench seat. Swift is quick, but is not the most gifted player in the game. Shortly after that match, Terry and I talked to Alun and suggested he joined Cardiff. I don't think he has regretted it, although at heart he is still a 'Jack'.

Another 'Jack' we have recruited is Gareth Roberts. He has proved to be a fine acquisition, and it was no surprise that Wales, albeit late in the day, picked him. I'm sure Gareth's best days are ahead of him, and that one day he could rank among the best flankers Wales have had in recent times. Bobby 'Larks' Lakin has been a Cardiff faithful since 1979, a product of our Youth team. He had in fact just been promoted from the Youth team when we toured South Africa in 1979. No blushing violet, Larks. In the match against North Free State at Sasolberg Cardiff made a hesitant start with the result that the 'Boks were running everything at us and put us under a lot of pressure. Suddenly, as I received the ball, I heard a squeaky voice. 'For f...'s sake, find touch' was the urgent message. It was Larks. The senior forwards in the side, including Scottie and Alan Phillips, turned their heads in disbelief. A Youth player daring to voice an opinion; didn't he know his place? We've been trying to keep Larks quiet ever since. It's an impossible task.

Another flanker, a really fine open-side, was Brian Lease. Brian put the optimum amount of work into every match, and possessed a lot of skill. He wasn't averse to going on the floor, either, but after he suffered a couple of nasty bouts of concussion, he quit the game. He was a great loss to Cardiff.

I'm told that Cardiff also have two good props, Ian Eidman and Jeff Whitefoot. I wouldn't know. Most of the time all I see of them is their backsides either going down for a scrum or disappearing completely in a ruck. I assume Bill and Ben, our nicknames for them, are making their presence felt. I'll have to talk to them about it one day, to find out what they actually do.

I see much more of Bobby 'Bungalow' Norster. At 6 ft 5 in, 16 st 7 lb you could hardly miss him, I suppose. Opposition line-out jumpers see a lot of him, too, and not many of them can boast that they've got the better of him. If someone kept statistics of clean line-out ball won, I'd bet the Bungalow would top the list in Britain. Holmesy and I have a telepathic understanding; Terry and Bobby have just as remarkable an affinity. He never seems to miss Holmesy with his feed from the line-out. For someone so precise, so clinical in his chief on-field activity Bobby is surprisingly half-soaked. Before Cardiff's match against the All Blacks in 1979, we had a lunch followed by a team-talk in the Angel Hotel. John Evans, then our coach, ended the session with a rousing call for action. 'Right', he said, 'Any questions? Has anyone got anything to say?'

Up jumped Bobby: 'I've forgotten my boots' he said, 'They're in Blaina.' Our coach couldn't believe it. The last thing any player would forget was his boots. Bobby would have to buy a new pair straight away, he ordered. No way, said Bobby. The only ones he could possibly wear were those he'd left at home in Blaina, some 30 miles away. The palaver of getting those boots defies description. Enough to say that someone was phoned in Newport, he rushed up the Western Valley to Blaina, and by incredible driving got Bobby's boots to the Arms Park ten minutes before kick-off. What would have happened if the boots hadn't arrived? Knowing Bobby, he'd have done a Zola Budd.

Just up the road from Blaina is a little village called Cwmcelyn, whose most famous product was David Watkins, the former Newport and Wales fly-half, that is until a rather large gentleman called Kevin Edwards came on to the scene. 'Heavy Kev' is a favourite with the Arms Park crowd because of his rumbustious runs straight at the opposition, who are either scattered like skittles or trampled underfoot. Kev takes as much stopping as a bull elephant. He's not subtle Kev, but effective. He has an unshakeable confidence in his own ability, as I once discovered quite accidentally. During Cardiff's tour of Zimbabwe in 1981, Kev found someone eager to listen to tales of his rugby exploits in a barber's shop in Bulawayo. He was waxing lyrical about his travels, his tours, his confidence that he'd be picked by Wales to tour South Africa in 1982 etc., when I walked into the shop for a trim. Kev was reclining in the barber's chair, his identity obscured by towels. I recognised the voice. I sat down and listened. Kev didn't notice me and continued with the rhetoric, the barber nodding and smiling, clearly delighted that he'd got a famous rugby player as a customer. I didn't say a word, but slipped away quietly. Later at the Team Court, I was prosecuting counsel. In front of everyone I charged Kev with over-confidence in his ability. 'Clearly guilty'. Kev squirmed in embarrassment. He hadn't a clue how I'd uncovered his secret.

Over the years, players have come and gone at Cardiff, but I'm not deceiving myself in believing the present squad is the best of the lot. As I suggested earlier in this chapter, Terry and I have a lot to be grateful for. Thanks lads. We appreciate it.

'England confides that every man will do his duty'

(Nelson's signal to the Fleet before the Battle of Trafalgar)

8
ENGLISHMEN ABROAD

It may be a somewhat romantic view that for 364 days of the year the average Welshman merely tolerates the Saeson – the Welsh word for the English – but that for 80 minutes or so on the 365th, alternately at Twickenham or the Arms Park, this sufferance is replaced by something altogether different. They become the 'enemy', a foe to be hated, and vanquished if possible in the grand manner, the natural riposte of the down-trodden and oppressed. Once the gesture has been made, and the victory has been won, it's back to normal: the English skulking away to lick their wounds and curse their ancestors while the Welsh return singing to the hills, valleys, the chapels, the mines and the farms, content once again that historical injustice has been partly redressed. A certain amount of smugness is understandable, particularly as Wales have beaten England on the rugby field more times than any other country.

In reality, things are different. I've found that the Welsh and the English get on very well together, in rugby terms, and that mutual respect abounds. There is a certain amount of harmless sniping whenever the countries play each other, but that's all part of the fun. As someone reared in an area in which grievances against the English were perhaps innate and justified, I have had to readjust my position and my attitudes over the years. What helped considerably in modifying my views of the English was that I was able to play with, and get to know, two of them at Cardiff. Barry Nelmes and John Scott may not be everyone's idea of archetypal Englishmen, but English they were and English they remained in a club which is Welsh to the core. I was very glad to have known them, to have played with them. It is enough to say they were Cardiff players.

Considering the number of top-class non-Welshmen who have played for Cardiff over the years, it is strange that Barry Nelmes was the first Englishman to be capped directly from the club. Barry joined Cardiff from Bristol in 1973, a year before me, and the same year that the 1985-86 captain, Alan Phillips, moved to us from Pyle. Barry was already a seasoned campaigner when he made his bid for a regular place in Cardiff's front row. The bulky and surprisingly mobile 17-stone West Countryman soon made his mark at loose-head prop, and by the end of the season he had gained his First XV cap along with Paul Evans, who had joined from Newport, John Luff, and my old pal, Brynmor Williams.

With Fran Cotton an automatic choice as England's loose-head (and sometimes tight-head), Nelmes was enough of a realist to accept that his best rugby would be played out for Cardiff. The fact that he was an Englishman playing for a senior Welsh club did not guarantee him pole position in England's selection stakes. As so often happens, however, fate played a part by dealing Barry a card from the bottom of the pack. Cotton was injured during the early part of England's ill-fated tour of Australia in 1975 and Barry was flown out to replace him. Nelmes won his first cap alongside five other debutants against Australia in Sydney. He won his second cap in a rough-house of a match at Brisbane, in which his Gloucestershire front row colleague, Mickey Burton, became the first Englishman to be sent off in an international match. Burton's 'crime', a late tackle, was greeted with some incredulity back in Britain, for Mickey had gained little in the way of reputation for tackling, late, early or otherwise.

Barry's pleasure at being capped, however, was somewhat muted. England lost both matches in Australia, and he soon found himself back on the list of also-rans even though Peter Colston, a former colleague of his at Bristol, was appointed to England's coaching duties for the following season. Coincidentally England's first match after their disappointing Australian tour was against Australia, at Twickenham, in January 1976. It was a match they desperately wanted to win, which explains why the old firm of Cotton and Burton were back. Beating Australia was about beating them up front. That meant no place for the mobile Nelmes and so, once again, he had to concentrate his mind on more mundane matters – namely aiding Cardiff, which he did with appreciable purpose and resolve until 1978, when England again acknowledged his abilities by inviting him back to international duty.

Barry's come-back match was England against Wales at Twickenham on 4 February – at first glance a match with little to recommend it, but which in retrospect can be viewed in a much more significant light. It turned out to be a match which dramatically altered the lives and careers of many.

Understandably, Nelmes' return to England duty was given rather less prominence in the rugby columns than the fact that his Cardiff colleague, Gareth Edwards, was to make his 50th appearance for Wales in the same match. There were reports of eight-pound stand tickets fetching £200 on the black market. That meant that some people at least had got their priorities wrong, because the match, played on a rain-sodden, heavy pitch was as depressing as the weather, dominated by the forwards and Edwards' line-kicking. The match was decided by kicks, Phil Bennett landing three penalties against two by Alistair Hignell.

However, as in all internationals there are things other than scores and results: there are matches within matches, private little wars and contests often unseen and sometimes unappreciated. Many believed, for instance, that England's new front row, which now included Nelmes, performed with credit against the Pontypool Front Row. This may have been the case, but Mickey Burton, villain or hero of the 1975 tour of Australia, depending on how you view it, never played for England again after this match.

Neither did Bob Mordell, the Rosslyn Park flanker. Bob was adjudged to have cost England the match by handling in a ruck near the English 25, Benny punishing the offence by kicking his third penalty. Mordell thus became a one-cap wonder, while his Rosslyn Park colleague, John Scott, who was making his second appearance for England, must have reflected on the cruelties of the game. An ambitious youngster then, Scottie was beginning to wonder in which direction his career lay and perhaps how to avoid a fate similar to Mordell's. His decision to quit English club rugby and join Cardiff had not yet been made. Uncertainty about the future also concerned the referee. Norman Sanson, acknowledged at that time as the outstanding referee in the world, was less than happy with the way the game at the top was being played. This was to be his last Championship match, though he did handle England in two other matches, against New Zealand, before he quit, depressed and disillusioned, in 1979.

Retirement was also beckoning other participants in the match, though few of us – particularly those of us who would be affected by such events – realised it. Edwards, Gerald Davies, captain of Cardiff, and Bennett would not be with us for the start of the 1978-79 season. My world, that of Nelmes, and of Scott, was suddenly about to be turned upside down and not one of us had an inkling of it. When there's an earthquake, the first you know of it is when the roof falls in on you.

Another interesting aspect of the match was that four Cardiff captains played in it: Gerald Davies, Edwards, Scott and Nelmes. Edwards was never appointed club captain of course but he did lead the club on several occasions. No doubt it will be appreciated by students of inconsequential fact that four 'bona fide' Cardiff captains, however, did play in the 1979 Wales versus England match: myself, Terry Holmes, Scottie and Alan Phillips. At the time of the 1978 match Scottie, as I've said, had not yet joined Cardiff, a move he was to make at the start of the next season. He was a Cardiff player by the time England played New Zealand at Twickenham on 25 November 1978. His new captain at Cardiff was Barry Nelmes and the vice-captaincy was vested in someone of more angelic countenance than either of them: yours truly.

Once again, these events were the upshot of the twists and turns of fate. Gerald Davies had been nominated as captain of Cardiff for the 1978-79 season but on his return from the tour of Australia, on which I gained my first Welsh caps, Gerald announced he was retiring from the game. Gerald's decision caught many by surprise for after all he was only 33 and had shown no appreciable loss of his nonpareil running skills. Gerald's decision not only left a yawning gap on the Wales wing, and one which probably has never been adequately filled, but left Cardiff without a captain. Nelmes, happy enough that he had been appointed vice-captain to Gerald, automatically succeeded him. Suddenly Nelmes had thrust upon him one of the most conspicuous honours the game has to offer, which I presume was consolation for the fact that England never called on him again after the end of the 1978 Championship. It seemed incredible too that as part of the general upheaval Barry's vice-captain was a relatively inexperienced 22-year-old from Tumble, which meant that, if tradition was adhered to, I was in line to succeed as captain of the world's most distinguished club.

All this was astonishing to me, particularly when I recall that one year earlier my career had seemed over before it had even begun. An Oxford specialist, having examined torn knee ligaments, determined that I would never play again. If I did, he said, I risked becoming a cripple for life. Yet within nine months of that chilling pronouncement I had won a Blue for Oxford at Twickenham, gained a first Welsh cap 'down under' in Australia, and become vice-captain of Cardiff. That's the stuff of fairy stories – I can still hardly believe that it happened.

Nelmes and Scott must ponder providence, too. Nelmes' philosophy that rugby should be an open, running game probably counted against him in terms of gaining further international recognition, but (reflecting the sharply differing attitudes in top rugby) it was that very philosophy which earned him the captaincy at Cardiff, where Gerald Davies, an exponent of 15-man rugby, ran the show and insisted upon similar thinking among his lieutenants. When Gerald quit, Nelmes was ready-made to take over – the Englishman who was welcome at the Arms Park but not at Twickenham.

Barry was a strange person really, sometimes distant and remote. I'm not sure he ever truly settled in at Cardiff, not because he was English in a Welsh club, or anything like that.

Like Gerald Davies he possessed an idealism about the way the game could or should be played, but unlike Gerald perhaps he found it hard to accept that sometimes Utopian visions can cloud over. When the January snows snarl down at Eugene Cross Park or the wind at Abertillery Park cuts you in two, and your forwards are battling for survival, you have to compromise a bit about the way you believe the game should be played. He probably has his reasons, but Nelmes hasn't bothered to keep in touch with the club. He still lives in Cardiff, running a pub. It seems a pity that he doesn't find the time to come down to the Arms Park these days, for a beer and a chit-chat about the good old days. I hope he is not one of those players who has gone out of the game with nothing but sadness and regret. There have been too many like that.

There was quite a contrast, in temperament and character, between Nelmes and Scott. John Philip Scott put so much passion, time and energy into playing for England that you'd swear he was a Welshman who'd taken the wrong turning, like Derek Morgan, of Newbridge. However, a more un-Welsh man than Scottie you couldn't expect to meet. When Scottie joined Cardiff from Rosslyn Park there must have been many sceptical of his ability to make the grade, even though he was already an England player. Although the former St Luke's College No. 8 had the physical attributes to play and survive on the most demanding club circuit in the world, there were understandable doubts in England and Wales alike regarding his skill, temperament and durability. Suffice it to say, Scottie eventually dispelled all the question marks, earning respect on every ground in Wales, though sometimes that respect had to be gained by giving new meaning to the catch-phrase 'bloodied but unbowed hero'. He gained his laurels the hard way, and I believe the experience made him a better player. The esteem in which he was held in Cardiff is summed up by the fact that he captained the club for four successive seasons, 1980-84.

Scott intimated that he wanted to join Cardiff during the Barbarians Easter tour of Wales in 1978. He scored a 50-yard try for the Baa-Baas against us at the Arms Park, and while I'm not sure whether that stupendous feat ensured the rolling out of the welcome carpet, it must have helped. There weren't many forwards of that sprinting capacity in Welsh rugby, let alone at Cardiff.

It was obvious from the start that Scottie wanted to make his presence felt at his new club. He seemed eager to promote the idea that he was one of nature's hard men, and that he was prepared to prove his macho image if any opposition forward had the inclination to take up the challenge. The rest of us waited if not with bated breath at least with something akin to fascination for the moment when someone would pick up the gauntlet thrown down by this brusquely competitive Englishman. We knew someone, soon, was bound to accept the brash challenge. It happened within a month of Scottie joining Cardiff, at Aberavon, which is no place for marshmallow men. Reputations are made and lost at the Talbot Athletic ground. Scottie made his, and at some cost. We backs, our minds naturally on other matters, are never certain how or why these things flare up, a flailing fist or belligerent boot usually indicating to us either the start or the finish of the action. On this occasion John Richardson, Aberavon's prop, did not take too kindly to a boot in the head. We have to presume Scott's name was at once mentally pencilled in John's 'black book', a hit list as notorious as it was long; and it was widely believed in Welsh rugby that big John had sworn to settle all accounts before he retired. In this event he did not wait long before remedying the indignity. After about ten minutes knuckle clashed with mouth and Scottie collapsed in a heap with blood pouring from his mouth with more profusion than it was from Richardson's hand. A dazed Scottie recovered after treatment and decided he was fit to play on but the referee seemed very concerned at the extent of Richardson's injury. 'Let's see your hand' he demanded. Shrewdly, John refused an examination. He needed treatment in the dressing-room, he declared, as he retired hastily in that direction. We discovered why at the end of the match, from Tom Holley, the Cardiff sponge-man. After treating Scottie, Tom had offered Richardson assistance and commiseration, and in the process was left in no doubt as to the ownership of two teeth firmly embedded in Richardson's hand. We never discovered what happened to the teeth. Scottie never did get back the couple that he mislaid.

This early baptism in the rigours of Welsh senior club rugby over, John settled down to prove himself a player as well. He did this without argument. He was a tremendous player in most aspects of forward play. Resolute, fearless and a superb tackler, he often added a new dimension to Cardiff's forward tactics. He was also a very good line-out player, though I thought he became less effective in this respect after having a couple of operations for ankle injuries. Personally, I considered his best matches for us were when circumstances required that he switched from No. 8 to lock. As a lock he'd arrive at the breakdown a little late, after, say, Owen Golding had won the ball but this made for an ideal situation because he'd take the ball on the charge. He was a brilliant ball-handler and when he was on a charge, he was nigh impossible to stop. It seems strange to suggest it, but Scottie shone more in the loose as a lock than as a No. 8, possibly because as a No. 8 he'd get to the ball and the flankers too soon to feed off them. He was always there, where it mattered, never afraid to go on the floor, and unflinchingly yielding to the risks: the kicks in the head, the rakings, and he accepted the bruises and gashes with little complaint.

Undoubtedly one of John's best matches was against Neath at the Gnoll in the 1985 season. We got hammered. None of us played very well – except Scottie. He was the only one who got stuck in. You'd think he was a survivor from the Gunfight at the OK Corral – he finished the match with six holes in his head. The odd thing about that match was that Neath didn't win it until they scored a remarkable breakaway try in injury time. It was one of my off days with the boot. If I had kicked successfully we'd have won, and we wouldn't have deserved to. After the match, Scottie made sure we were all aware of his sacrifice. The details of each cut, every stitch, were imparted. He loves that, showing off his injuries. It's a fetish with him.

Another of his quirks is his inability to keep a secret. There are plenty of occasions these days when rugby men are involved in something hush-hush. The rule is 'don't tell Scottie', otherwise everybody will know before the week is out. Discretion is not part of his make-up. A good example of this was when he, Terry Holmes and myself were figuring in negotiations for a trip to South Africa. Let's say they centred on a European XV playing there. Naturally, everybody involved had reasons to keep the plans for the trip under cover. But what happened? After a couple of clandestine meetings with the interested parties, there was Scottie blabbing in the Cardiff dressing-room about a trip to South Africa.

When looked at in isolation, these quirks suggest a basic insecurity. So too does his abrasiveness with people. A spade is never a gardening implement with John. He speaks his mind forcefully, often rudely. People generally do not like this side of his character. In fact when he first came to Cardiff, everyone hated him. His chat was like his play, blunt and uncompromising. I think I've got to know him reasonably well over the years. I like him. He's a guy you could rely on to do something for you, if you asked. But knowing him and knowing him well are two different matters. He has this roundabout way of dealing with everyone. You just can't pin him down to a straight 'yes' or 'no'. You can only come to the conclusion that really it is all a front, a cover for the fact that basically he may be a very shy and self-conscious person.

In my first few years at Cardiff, there was barrier, a rift, between committee and players. Communication was difficult because there seemed to be little in common between the two elements. I wouldn't care to comment on the reason for this; but Scottie soon made it his business to try to change things. His technique was hardly out of the diplomatic manual. Verbal abuse poured over various committee men. He was highly critical of all and sundry – some very prominent officers were often invited to 'P... off', and similarly phrased suggestions had some players scuttling away fearful of the consequences. The abuse was aimed at trying to make Cardiff a players' club and at reminding the powers that be that the players were the sole reason they belonged to the club. I firmly believe that Scottie's extraordinary approach was the reason that committee and players eventually gelled. It's remarkable though that he got away with it, for Cardiff have a tradition of powerful and influential committee men. Many lesser players, I'm sure, would have been peremptorily kicked out of the club. Scottie probably escaped such dismissal because under him the club prospered: we had excellent team spirit, a lot of good players had joined us, we achieved a high standard of play, and, above all, we were a winning side. Under Scottie's leadership Cardiff won the Welsh Cup three times in four years, an achievement which distinguished him from many other previous captains.

This is not to say that Scottie was a good captain. In fact, he was dreadful, hopeless really. He led by example on the field, which is important, but in all other respects he did not measure up to the players' ideas of a good captain. Part of the problem was self-created. Being the kind of person he was, you could never take him seriously, so when he attempted, say, at team talks to adopt a stern, thoughtful approach nobody believed him. We often suspected an ulterior motive. His other technique, much more plausible, was to mess about, mixing jibes and ridicule. Neither worked. Having suggested that the committee men were exasperated by him, and really did not know how to cope with him, the players had to treat him differently. Although a fine player, his tactical understanding of the game was limited. His forceful personality meant that we succumbed to at least trying out his suggestions on the playing side. We simply felt we were obliged to do so, even if deep down we were all saying to ourselves 'he's talking a lot of balls'. Holmesy and myself, in comparison, were less forceful in our presentation of ideas, and we often got the response 'we don't agree with that'. That never happened to Scottie. Having a lot of good players around him, of course, made a difference: decisions were made for him, which disguised his inadequacy in that respect.

Still, for all that he was popular and well liked by the players, and not just because he was such a fine player. Although no-one could ever be certain what he would say, he was appreciated greatly for instance in the way he dealt with selection. He was blunt, certainly, but he was straight. He would tell somebody to his face the reason for his non-selection. It would be 'you're not picked, you're not good enough' or 'you're not playing well at the moment'. Scottie would never hide behind platitudes. He would never say 'I voted for you, but everyone else didn't'. How much better the rugby world would be if all selectors were as candid.

I've no doubt that although he has achieved most of the honours the game has to offer his greatest disappointment is that he was never a British Lion. A lot of top players also missed out in this respect, some because of eccentricity in selection, others simply because they were unlucky enough to be around when another player was supreme. Scottie fell into another category – he was a victim of unusual, even bizarre circumstances. For years now he has been at loggerheads with Jeff Squire, the Pontypool and Wales back row forward. To say they have no love or regard for one another would be to understate the situation. The root of it I do not know. Possibly something occurred between them when they were at college together at St Luke's, but whatever it was it has festered. Ultimately it proved to be the reason that Scottie did not go on the 1980 Lions tour to South Africa. Scottie was certainly a candidate for selection – many believed in fact that as part of England's Grand Slam side he was the front runner. His cause was undermined after England had beaten Wales at Twickenham in the notorious 'Paul Ringer' match. At the after-match banquet, Syd Millar, the Lions manager, came up to a group of the Welsh team, including Squire and myself. Jeff and I at the time were very friendly and enjoyed each other's company. The conversation, hardly surprisingly, moved on to selections for the forthcoming Lions tour. Discussion hovered on who should and should not go, Jeff's opinion obviously being respected by Millar, because at the time Jeff was probably Britain's most senior forward and an automatic choice to tour. Names came and went and Scottie's eventually cropped up. Jeff did not pull any punches: 'Well, if he's going, I'm not. Count me out' he told Millar. Scottie did not go. Jock Beattie and Derek Quinnell got the vote ahead of him.

Scottie was overlooked again in 1983, when Willie John McBride's Lions toured New Zealand. It's possible that the 'Squire syndrome' once again prevailed, for after the Lions had persuaded Squire to tour – he had originally said he could not – there might have been no room for Scottie for the same reason as in 1980. It did not help his candidature that England had not done well that season, nor that Scottie had in fact played ordinarily even for Cardiff. Even so, it was a wretched situation that someone of his ability should be deprived of one of the game's major honours.

'It's always the season for the old to learn'

Aeschylus

9
1956 AND ALL THAT

I'm an occasional visitor to a pub in Llandaff called the Butcher's Arms, which is a popular watering-hole for Cardiff players of varying vintage. The Butcher's' reputation is based on good ale and conviviality, but no doubt most Arms Parkers call there because the 'guvnor' is Derek Williams. Derek, better known as C.D., is a former chairman of Cardiff. A flanker with a reputation for fire and commitment, C.D. won two caps and, if you surrender to the nostalgic persuasion of some of his contemporaries, you can begin to believe he was unlucky not to have won more.

The unusual thing about C.D.'s brief international career is that both appearances were against France, and Wales won each time. In the first match, at the old Stade Colombes, in 1955, Wales won by 16-11, a then record score against France in France. The French are hardly likely to forget it for, having beaten Scotland, Ireland and England, they were understandably confident that they would achieve their first-ever Grand Slam. The back row opposition on that occasion were of the highest calibre – Domec, Celaya and Jean Prat – and C.D. could be justified in claiming that he helped see them off. This was certainly true of Prat, one of the great French forwards of all time. 'Monsieur Rugby', as Jean was known, never played for France again, his eight-year international career ending a few months before his 32nd birthday. C.D. blighted the life of the French even more markedly the following season. It was his try at the Arms Park, converted by Garfield Owen, that enabled Wales not only to win 5-3 but to take the Championship for the third season in a row. Some controversy surrounded

C.D.'s try: the French were convinced that he had grounded the ball over the dead-ball line. Dr Cooper, the English referee, deemed otherwise to enable C.D. to carve a special niche in the history of the game.

The reader may wonder why it is that I seem well-versed in the details of C.D.'s era, apart from the fact that it was clearly an outstanding period in Welsh rugby history. I hasten to add that it is not the result of 'all our yesterdays' sessions in the Butcher's, although there have been plenty of those, and revealing they have been. The reason is much simpler: 1956, the year of C.D.'s try, held some special importance for me too. It was the year I was born. It is a fascinating exercise, I find, to look back to 1956 and make comparisons with modern-day rugby. You can come to some surprising conclusions.

Take Wales for instance. Even though they were blessed with an outstanding side – good enough as I've said to win the Championship for a third season in a row – they weren't exactly scoring sensations. In fact Wales' points haul from four Championship matches in 1956 was 25, which was made up of six tries (then valued at 3 points), two conversions and a penalty by Garfield Owen. If Wales didn't manage to score that number of points in *one* match today there would be an outcry. The team would have failed. Yet put into perspective, that 25-point aggregate was the lowest by a team winning the Five Nations Championship, save for Ireland's 21 points in 1951 and England's 25 points in 1930. It is not for me to criticise that 1956 Welsh side for their paucity in scoring – I refer to them merely to establish a comparison with modern Welsh sides, and to underline how differently the scoring of points is regarded today. If you don't score a hatful of points, even the barman stops calling you sir.

As a lad I grew up with tales of the players of that era, wonderful players who could perform miracles on the rugby field, who made brave men cry with their valiant deeds, and who won the undying respect of those that watched them represent their country. They would make up a Rugby Who's Who on their own – in Wales we had Cliff Morgan, Ken Jones, Malcolm Thomas. England had Jeff Butterfield, W.P.C. Davies,

Peter Jackson, Jeeps and Cannell. Scotland's superstars included Arthur Smith and Angus Cameron. Ireland, too, had players who were household names: Jackie Kyle, Tony O'Reilly and Cecil Pedlow. France boasted Maurice Vannier, Jean Dupuy, André Boniface and Georges Dufau. What marvellous players they all were, we were told, full of flair, imagination, pace and purpose. They could cut openings like knives through butter, making defenders shrivel in embarrassment. Great players all. Heroes to a man.

Yet I cannot help feeling how extraordinary it is that, for all their consummate skill, these former players, who captivated the crowds from the Arms Park to Murrayfield, apparently possessed one serious defect – a relative inability to score points or make scores for their colleagues. No matter whether it was in obtaining tries, conversions, dropped goals or penalties, the revered players of the past compare substantially less favourably in all respects with the modern points-scorers. The common explanation for this gulf is that players of the past had to contend with tighter defences, and that scoring opportunities were consequently fewer. Tighter defences than today? I'm sceptical about that. Why is it that some contemporary players have scored more points in ten minutes than many past immortals did in a season – or in a lifetime, in some cases – and that some of them have found themselves on the bench for the following match, wondering what they have done wrong? It seems a paradox to me that the players of the past were so good, yet they did not come up to the mark in one of the most important aspects of rugby.

The lack of scoring was not confined to international matches, either. It may not be of riveting importance, but it makes for an interesting comparison that the 383 points I scored out of 1,214 for Cardiff in 1983-84, both club records, amounted to more than half the club's total points in the 1955-56 (612 points in 52 matches) and 1956-57 (627 in 50) seasons – and I played in only 35 matches. In my first season at Cardiff, 1975-76, I scored 232, which passed the previous record by John Davies (209 in 1972-73), and the fact that I have come close to nearly doubling that figure since is an indication of the high scoring that Cardiff supporters now witness and expect. Lovers of statistics might also be interested in the fact that since Cardiff's first season in 1876 there have been 23 seasons in which the club total was actually lower than my personal tally in 1983-84.

Cardiff clearly struggled in scoring terms after 1956, for only once in seven seasons did they top 500: in fact twice they finished with under 400. From then on, however, an upward trend in scoring was discernible, culminating in their first four-figure total, 1,058 points in 1971-72. It should be emphasised, I think, that this trend embraced *all* forms of scoring, not just the much-maligned penalty kick. That year Cardiff scored 175 tries, a total previously bettered only in the 1947-48 season, which was exceptional in every respect: 39 wins, 803 points and 182 tries from 41 matches. The advance still goes on. Modern Cardiff players continue to outstrip their predecessors at all methods of points-scoring with 192 tries in 1983-84 the peak. Curiously Cardiff lost ten matches that season. Fortunately they can't blame me – I played in only two of those defeats, against Llanelli and Pontypool. It was part of my job to keep that scoring momentum. I certainly got off to a flying start with 100 points from the first eight matches. I finished that extraordinary season with 82 conversions (another record), though probably more relevant was the number of tries that were converted, for I played only 35 times. I wasn't scoring that many tries myself, but it is important to specify that the club were. A conversion, a dropped goal and the odd penalty goal are usually significant only in close matches. When you are a pile of points in front early in a match there is a danger of slackening off and of playing loose, uninspiring rugby. At Cardiff, our fastidious crowd appreciate a tight, well-contested match but obviously prefer it when we finish with a scoring flourish. The period before we 'turn on' quite often determines how we play in the final 20 minutes. The psychology of scoring would make a fascinating case study for someone. I have no set views on the subject: for one thing, I'm not sure which is best remembered – the kick that goes over and wins a match, or the one that misses to lose it. It's a classic Catch 22.

I have been asked often whether I have deliberately set out to break scoring records. The answer is no. I failed my 'A' Level Maths, which may illustrate the difficulty I have with figures. I'm none too bright when it comes to records either. There have been many times when my ignorance of a record has proved positively embarrassing, and I have to rely for details on the good offices of journalists like John Kennedy, Paul Rees and John Billot, who have willingly supplied information whenever I have required it. Having said that I haven't set out to break records, I suppose I have to admit to having had a go at one Cardiff record – Barry John's four dropped goals in a match, which he scored against Llanelli on 28 November 1970. That was a matter of family pride. B.J.'s uncle, Joe Morgan, who lives a few doors away from my father in Tumble, had a penchant for comparing B.J. and myself, and our respective scoring careers. My father was easily enticed. The banter with Joe, usually across the garden fence, became a matter of quite intense if friendly rivalry between them, as did the size of their cabbages. B.J. had done this, B.J. had done that, Joe needled away. 'You wait and see, my boy' Dad would respond, taking the bait as Joe knew he would. So whenever I did something which Dad reckoned compared favourably with B.J. like breaking the Cardiff scoring record, he was immediately down the garden to let Joe know all about it. 'What about *that* then?' Joe was not so easily outdone. 'Well, there's one record he *won't* break and that's Barry's four dropped goals.' Dad's confidence was astounding: 'Wanta bet, good boy, wanta bet?'. It was all very Welsh, and very amusing, except that it put some pressure on me because, for the only time in his life, my father suddenly wanted desperately for me to achieve something in sporting terms. That's where family pride came in. I felt I simply had to try to keep Davies ahead of Morgan in the badinage. Duty it was, wasn't it? Talk about keeping up with the Jones's . . .

Now, it's all very well wanting to do something, but often another matter to achieve it. The trouble with drop kicks is that you never go out on to the field with the intention of dropping one, let alone four. Dropped goals are spontaneous acts or frequently reactions. You could go through a career and never try more than two in a match. As luck would have it, I had a chance to go for B.J.'s record quite early on, in 1981, when, having dropped three goals against Pontypool at the Arms Park, it occurred to me that here was the golden opportunity. Dad's bet could be on. I *had* to have a go for a fourth. I did. And I missed. 'That's it,' I thought, 'I'll never get another chance'. Two years later I did. This time it was against Swansea, at the Arms Park on 3 December 1983, a match of imperishable memory because I played in it with the biggest hangover of my life. The night before I had attended my office party and, like a good rugby player should on the eve of a match, I sensibly stuck to orange juice – at least I did for the first two drinks. I'm hazy as to why or how I moved on to wine, but it is enough to say that I partook liberally. It was probably the orange juice, but the next day I felt absolutely dreadful . . . and I had to play in the afternoon, against Swansea, and against Malcolm Dacey, deadly rivals both. In my fragile condition, the prospect held about as much appeal as diving into a shark-infested pool, or attending a Welsh squad session. As it happened the wine (or the orange juice) must have contained some magical ingredient. I played tolerably well, and with a lovely service from Steve Cannon, Cardiff won and I dropped four goals. I'd have loved to have been down the garden back home the next day and to have seen Dad's moment of triumph, but you can't have everything, can you? I have been pressed since as to why I didn't try to break Barry's record and attempt a fifth. In truth there wasn't enough time left in the match. I could also have been influenced by the feeling that by then the crowd was beginning to find the exercise tedious, to say the least. They'd much rather have seen Mark Ring score again to make his hat-trick of tries, I'm sure.

By the strangest of coincidences, I equalled the four-dropped-goal feat against Pontypool at the start of the 1985-86 season on 16 October at Pontypool Park. Cardiff were attacking Pontypool's ground record of 49 straight wins, and I must say I thought when my fourth kick went over five minutes from the end we had pulled off a notable achievement. But Pontypool, as they often do, found something in reserve and ironically their fly-half Mike Goldsworthy dropped a goal right at the end to give his side a 13-12 win.

Although I have a fairly indifferent attitude to dropped goals, I take some pleasure in the fact that I hold the Cardiff record, which was 53 dropped goals at the end of the 1984-85 season. The chief reason is that it brackets me with some very illustrious former Cardiff players, not least that audacious little fly-half Percy Bush whose 35 dropped goals in 14 seasons between 1900 and 1914 stood for so long as one of the club's most revered achievements. Only two players came close to Percy's feat – Wilf Wooller and Barry John. They each scored 30. Wooller, incidentally, holds the record for a season with 13, but special mention must also go to Gareth Edwards. He dropped 24 goals, which is a rare accomplishment for a scrum-half, a position which by its very nature offers limited scope for drop shots. But then Gareth was ever the supreme opportunist.

Obviously there was a different attitude to drop-kicking in the old days, and not merely because the kick was worth four points as opposed to today's three. Scoring then was relatively light, and the snap dropped goal could win or lose a match in which one try and a couple of penalty goals was a typical product of 80 minutes' play. In fact, in Wooller's case the dropped goal became an essential part of his and Cardiff's scoring repertoire. It may even have been a forerunner of set-move play, for Wilf – who was a centre, remember – had a 'right' and 'wrong' call which required that the scrum-half delivered the ball straight to him so that he could have a go at a dropped goal. (The 'wrong' call, incidentally, was the 'right' one, a shout to confuse the opposition.) Wilf explains that the importance of the dropped goal in his day was chiefly as a counter to very tight, flat defences, and that for someone like him, who could drop-kick from a very long way out, the appeal of having a go regularly was obvious. By all accounts, Wilf was a superb kicker of the bigger, heavier ball that they used to play with. Another of his ploys was to deliberately punt the ball dead from his own half, for players discerned ready advantage in thereby forcing the defending side to drop out from the 25-yard line. Wilf played for Cambridge in three 'Varsity Matches, 1933 to 1935, and students of that match still acclaim one of his dropped goals, a towering 55-yarder which went through the posts like a howitzer shell and landed on the first row of seats of the (then) South Terrace during Cambridge's 29-4 win in 1935.

Wilf's enormous power as a kicker was clearly an advantage to him, but it is interesting that he was not averse to practice, unusual though his methods were. During his days as a schoolteacher, he'd find an empty classroom and practise and practise to perfect the release and contact. The timing was essential and the ball had to come off the hard floor at just the right angle if he was to complete the action and thump the ball against the wall. He has never disclosed how many times window panes in the classroom had to be replaced. Wilf, incidentally, bemoans the present parlous state of Welsh rugby. It is intriguing that though our playing careers are 50 years apart, we find ourselves in agreement over at least one aspect of the game: it is essential that methods should be found to improve passing and handling skills. His idea that all matches be suspended for the whole of one month, say October or November, and the time given over to passing practice certainly strikes me as a provocative one, and is not as outlandish as it may appear.

A footnote on that 1956-57 season: Cardiff's first match was against West Germany and their next Italy. They had a victory either side of my birthday. In January they played and beat South African Universities and they finished what must have been their most cosmopolitan season by touring Romania. Oh, I almost forgot. At Easter the Barbarians came to the Arms Park and won 40-0, which was the biggest defeat ever suffered by Cardiff. As someone once said, you can't win them all.

'A man must make his opportunity, as oft as find it'

Francis Bacon

as 'Nasty' Botha, the Springbok fly-half, seems happy enough even though two penalty goals
n yours truly enabled Cardiff to beat his side, Pretoria Police, at Loftus Versfeldt in May 1982.

Above: That old morning-after feeling. Yours truly looking appropriately sorry for himself aft dislocating a shoulder in the Lions' first match of the tour, against Eastern Province at Port Elizabeth in 1980. I played in four matches on that ill-starred tour, and was injured in two of then

Top right: The St John's Ambulancemen seem more concerned about my bloody nose than t leg injury I suffered playing for the British Lions in the Second Test against South Africa at Bloemfontein in 1980, an injury which ended my tour. *Colorsport*

Right: The walking wounded homeward bound. W.D.G., Dai Richards, Terry Holmes and Fr Cotton try to wear brave faces as we say goodbye to the British Lions in South Africa in 1980, ea of us ruled out of taking further part in the tour because of injury. *Colorsport*

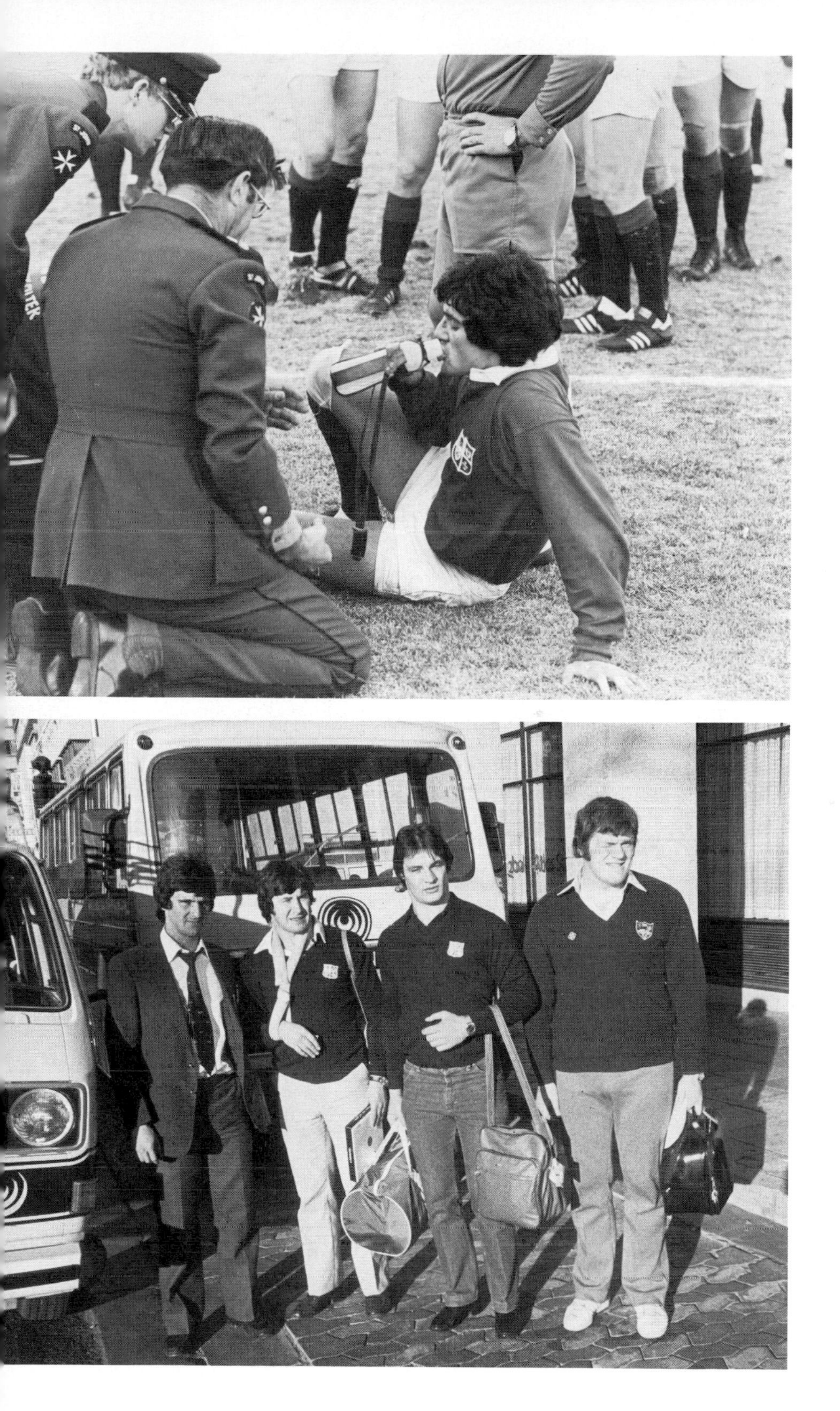

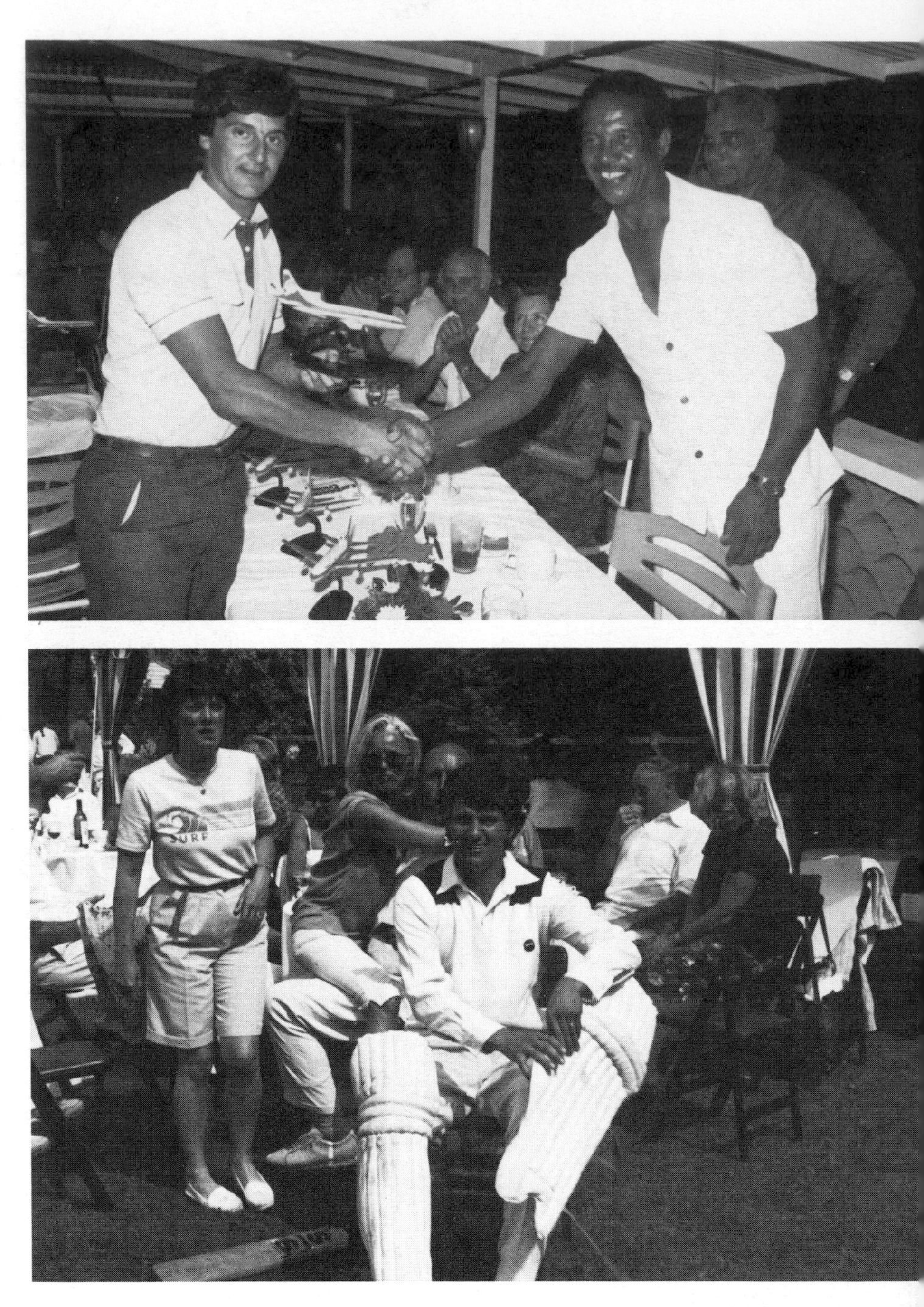

Top: Meeting my sporting hero. Sir Garfield Sobers presents a trophy to me as a member of David Gower XI which won a Pro-Am cricket tournament in Barbados in November 1983. Th previous time I had seen Sobers was when he hit Glamorgan's Malcolm Nash for six sixes in over at St Helen's in 1972.

Above: If you haven't played cricket in Paris you haven't lived. Here I am, with Helen at hand, a Colleen and Fred Rumsey behind, waiting to bat for the Lord's Taverners against a French X which included Pierre Villepreux, a better rugby player than he proved to be a cricketer. T same might be said of me.

Top: A natural break during a serious round of golf in the Welsh Rugby Union's Pro-Am at St Pierre, Chepstow, in 1984. Shrewdly, Barry John and Windsor Davies keep some distance between me and Malcolm Dacey, my then arch-rival for the Wales fly-half position. One thing is certain – I'm a better golfer than Malcolm.

Above: Another game which I enjoy – squash. *Colorsport*

Left: A cack-handed 6-iron to the heart of the green (I think), at St Pierre in 1984.

Above: Colin Patterson looks on approvingly as I make the acquaintance of a local at the dolphinarium at Port Elizabet shortly before the Lions opened their 1980 campaign in Sou Africa.

Left: Another obligatory photo call on a Lions tour. The lion c wasn't that interested in the visitors to Vanderbijl Park, whe we spent a week's acclimatisation an hour from Johannesbu

Top right: The finger and the high brow belong to Jim Renwi W.G.D. getting in some early duty at Windhoek, my first ma back after injury. Is this what Scottie means by 'laid back'? *Bob Thomas*

Right: Nick Youngs, the England scrum-half, gives a good impression of being pleased that I've scored a try for the Western Province President's Centenary XV against Weste Province at Newlands in 1983. Behind Nick is Mark 'Cowbo Shaw, the All Black flanker cum No. 8. *Bob Thomas*

Now that I've become a Barbarian committee man, I wonder if I'll ever be invited to wear one o
these jerseys again. *Bob Thomas*

10
INSIDE NUMBER TEN

One of the qualities of rugby football, and possibly the reason for its success as a team sport, is that it allows anyone to play, regardless of his shape, size, weight, pace or skill. Generally the individual's configuration will determine the position in which he plays, and if he accepts a certain position as a youngster, because of his shape, the likelihood is that he will specialise in it and be faithful to it for the rest of his playing career. He will only swap positions if he becomes correspondingly slower, quicker, heavier or taller. In the case of the fly-half, however, the determining factor has little to do with shape. A player becomes a fly-half because someone, usually an ex-player, a teacher, makes the decision for him, the deciding factor being a range of skills the youngster possesses which others do not. It really doesn't matter whether he is tall, short, slim or stocky. Once a youngster is indoctrinated into the fly-half position he rarely switches to another one, except for reasons of expedience or to comply with irrational selection.

It follows, of course, that a lot of schoolboys are disappointed, particularly in Wales, when someone determines they are not skilled enough to get the chance to emulate their heroes, like Barry John or Phil Bennett: 'You, boy, you play tight-head prop', or 'Evans, you can't pass – get on the wing'. Conversely, the boy who can beat an opponent, is a good handler and passer, and who can kick naturally is a prime candidate for the No. 10 jersey. With these attributes it is reckoned he is equipped to be the most dominant player in the side, a decision-maker.

I have a theory that unless these skills are inherent, naturally part of the youngster's make-up, there is little chance of his succeeding at the highest level. The ability has got to be there at the start, for in the normal evolution of things there will be no opportunity to acquire it later. A prime example of this is Dai Richards, the Swansea centre. Originally Dai was a fly-half, and a very good one, because he could beat an opponent and was an excellent handler and giver of a pass. Dai's problem was his inability to kick very well, and while he was able to disguise this fault in his game in the early part of his career, it became a handicap later. He worked tremendously hard on improving his kicking, but because he didn't have a natural talent for it, he never really succeeded. Most of the fly-half's kicking is done under pressure, and your reactions must be quick, instinctive. No amount of practice can compensate for the lack of this ability. Dai's switch to centre, where kicking is less important, became inevitable.

In my own case, I had to practise interminably to improve my natural ability as a kicker. I spent more time at school in improving my kicking than on any other part of my game. As a consequence, my kicking is now entirely instinctive. To some it appears a little too casual, too natural. A criticism I do resent, however, is that I'm a kicking fly-half. Although kicking is an integral part of a fly-half's repertoire, I can't think of any fly-half who kicks *less* in a match than I do. Perhaps I've a reputation as a kicker because generally I'm able to kick further than most other fly-halves; it seems to frustrate the opposition and annoy their fans when I bang one a long way into touch.

This gives me leave, I think, for digression. Although rugby has a reasonably good record in crowd behaviour, the attitude of some so-called fans is reprehensible. Partisanship, loyalty to the home team, is acceptable and understandable, but there always seems to be an element among those supporters which is downright vindictive and nasty, almost to the point of being violent. By nature tolerant, I usually shrug it off. But there have been times when the verbal abuse has been sickening, leaving me to wonder what the game is all about, and whether indeed it was worth my continuing playing. Once or twice I have reacted and retorted with the old Harvey Smith. Lately, though, I have mellowed. A smile works wonders. Still, the verbal ruffians should look at themselves, and question their motives. They should realise that when all is said and done, rugby players are only on the park to enjoy themselves and hopefully to entertain. The bitter, over-intense support in rugby – and in other sports – should not be allowed to prevail.

The modern fly-half often is faced with a greater dilemma than whether he should pass, run or kick. He is the decision-maker, but too often the decision he should be making is predetermined by set moves. If a set move is called, obviously the fly-half must join in with it, even though instinctively he may feel it is the wrong thing to do. Today it takes courage and firmness to over-call a set move and do your own thing. A fly-half worth his salt should decide if a called move is still on by examining the evidence: has the ball carried from the scrum-half? Is the ball quick enough? Is it in the right place at the point of take so that he can pass easily?

Another important task for the fly-half is to assess the opposition's strength and weaknesses. For instance, is the full-back secure under a high ball? Does the open-side wing come inside and commit himself in defence or does he stay out, which may mean there is room for our full-back to come into the attack and probe the space? It is also important to assess whether the opposition defence shuffles in midfield – that is, do they float across the field? One way to counter this is to run straight; the fly-half could try a direct break himself, or work a scissors with his inside centre to try to wrong-foot the defence. I have found for example that when the opposition centres are lying up flat, the 'miss move' is worth trying. The fly-half should always be alert to the opposition's defence: many matches are won by exposing their weaknesses.

It is not only for diplomatic reasons that a fly-half should also always think of his forwards' welfare. You must not take things for granted. If, for instance, the pack is doing well in the set-pieces, don't just let them get on with it or call out 'well done, lads'. No matter how dominant they may be it is not advantageous to have them running all over the park. They need a breather now and then, and it is sound game-planning to tighten things up for five minutes or so.

The fly-half is important as the pivot of the team, his influence crucial, and it is not readily appreciated that he must have greater powers of concentration than any other player in the side. It is one of the most difficult parts of the job, and it has probably been my weakness. I get bored far too easily, I lose interest. This usually happens in high-scoring matches, and explains why I rarely take advantage when my side has scored a shovelful. Once the game has been won, instead of being eager for the ball I admit to becoming lackadaisical. I languish, waiting for the final whistle. A match in 1983, in which I played for Cardiff at Ebbw Vale, is a case in point. We had scored a lot of points when, five minutes into the second half, I turned to 'Pablo' Rees, our full-back, and said: 'Hey Pablo, Billy's in'. Pablo scoured the terraces for Billy. He looked puzzled. 'Billy Boredom' I shouted the explanation. Pablo dissolved in laughter. This attitude would never do in the bigger matches. They bring out the best in players – including me. The closer the score, the greater the concentration. There are few places to hide if you make one mistake and lose the match.

One of the areas of my game which I have worked hard on during recent years is defence. I have to admit that defence in my early days was conspicuous by its absence, but as I have gained in experience, I have come to realise, for instance, the value of a fly-half coming up in defence, not so much to tackle, but to strengthen the defensive line. At Cardiff years ago, I used to implore Stuart Lane to come back and cover for me, and like the excellent open-side he was, Stuart often did just that. That sort of thing wouldn't be accepted by our flankers today.

I remember discovering that there is more to defending than meets the eye when I played for Cardiff against Pretoria Defence in South Africa. One of the opposition forwards was 'Moaner' Van Heerden, the renowned giant lock-forward, and his speciality was to peel from the line-out and run straight at the opposing fly-half. He was a fearsome sight, and when he employed his tactic from the first line-out of the match, I froze with fright. Fortunately, Mike Murphy, our centre, found the courage to cut across in front of me and tried to bring the giant down. Poor Mike was flattened, knocked out. He woke up in Pretoria Royal Infirmary. Ten minutes later, Moaner roared from the line-out again, straight towards me. This time, there were no Cardiff heroes. It was up to me! My reaction was survivalist rather than instinctive. As Moaner was on the point of head-on impact, I leaned backwards, with the result that Moaner not only fell over me, but lost possession as he smashed to the ground. From that moment I earned a new nickname – 'Bonecrusher Davies'. Now, whenever I have to tackle a big man head on, this is the method I adopt – and recommend.

Another aspect of my game developed in the last four years or so is running straight, essentially to commit the open-side flanker and the opposing fly-half. It does not necessarily produce gaps in the defence, but its virtue is that the opposing fly-half has to stop to take me and, if his centres have continued to shuffle across, there will be space for my inside centre to take advantage. It also allows the alternative of linking inside with the back row. Above all, a straight running foray by the fly-half introduces doubt in the defence, and quite often prevents the shuffle happening too quickly. The fly-half who runs laterally is very easy to defend against, and such running makes his whole back division easy to defend against.

Not many fly-halves contemplate making breaks from set-pieces. Phil Bennett, for example, rarely did so, although his devastating running from the loose play amply compensated for it. (Benny, incidentally, was always a charitable player on the field, always ready to say 'well done' to friend and opponent alike.) Of those that do, I suppose that John Rutherford of Scotland, and young Jonathan Davies are the best known exponents. My defence against a set-piece break is to try to line up on the opposing fly-half's outer shoulder. This leaves room for an attempt at a break inside – where the back row would be expected to gobble him up – but also helps my centres to shuffle across and block the full-back or extra man if the fly-half decides to move the ball instead.

There is no doubt that my game has developed because I had the advantage of playing with some great scrum-halves, notably Gareth Edwards, Brynmor Williams and Terry Holmes.

All of them were long passers, and it may seem heretical to say it, but some of my best games were because my scrum-half passed short and quickly. With Holmesy, for instance, we often would agree that for ten minutes or so, I would take every ball short. We employed this as a variation, and we found that it had the effect of tying down the opposing flanker, and making the opposition think.

If I decided that a long diagonal kick would be useful, generally I would ask Terry for a long pass, wide enough to give me more time to welly the ball away. When I wanted to have a crack at a break, or I'd spotted a disrupted back division, I'd suggest a sharp and short pass. The long diagonal has two effects. The first is that if it gains touch, either your forwards are encamped in opposing territory, or it has meant you have relieved pressure in your own half which also disheartens the side who have worked hard to get there in the first place. The second consequence can be just as important. By anticipating the long kick, the full-back would often have to lie deep and very wide. In so doing he triggers off options for our backs, and if a break is made, the defending full-back would be way out of position. A full-back gambles positionally every time he faces a long kicking fly-half.

The drop kick is another useful weapon employed by the fly-half. It is a great psychological boost, personally and for the team, if you can pop one over early in the match. It may sound far-fetched, but I cannot recall losing a match after I have dropped an early goal. Generally, I seem to try to drop goals only in important matches, although I've been known to have a go simply because of a bet in a pub the previous week or to help my father win a few over-the-back-fence arguments. This may explain why I am the Cardiff dropped goal record-holder. The important part of the drop kick – as indeed with the punt – is the release. The ball must not change in line from the time it is released to the time it is kicked. This is the reason why kicking in the wind is so difficult. With the wind against, it blows the ball as it is released. Wind 'advantage' can also be problematic, because it can change the position of the ball between the time of release and impact.

The most important part of punting is finding touch. It is relatively easy to punt short and safe, but I'm easily tempted, as I am in golf, to say: 'Let's go for the big one'. In golf, when the big one goes wrong, you have only yourself to blame. In rugby, 14 angry glares give you another message. When the big one comes off – the 3-wood across the water, the 70-yarder that floats over the touch-line – you feel very pleased with yourself. However, it must be remembered that many a big match has been won or lost because of a missed late kick to touch. In the last match of the 1977 Lions tour of New Zealand, the Lions were beaten because Phil Bennett, one of the great touch-finders, failed near the end, the All Blacks followed an up and under, and Laurie Knight scored the winning try.

Although the fly-half is usually the best kicker in the side, goal-kicking itself is not a fly-half skill. To be an accomplished goal-kicker therefore is a bonus. My ratio of successful place-kicks has increased dramatically over the past three years, and this has had a marked effect on the number of points I have scored. From just over 200 points a season, my total has shot up to near the 400 mark in the last two. I put it down to a better attitude of mind, although it may also be linked with my increasing interest in golf. In golf you must be confident, you must be slow, your timing spot on. The rules apply precisely to place-kicking. There is no need for brute force. I'm sure it has also helped that I have practised a lot more in the past three years than I did in the previous three or four. There is not much time in coaching sessions to get in kicking practice, and so I've had to make time, either by arriving early or staying later. It's a lonely occupation, often, and probably the best thing to do is to find a youngster who you can bribe with socks or shorts so that he will act as ball-boy. It's hardly any wonder I'm always running out of kit.

Overall, the most important aspect of fly-half play is having a positive attitude, being confident. A negative approach means you won't try things and there is no encouragement to the backs outside you. But when your confidence is flowing, and you are playing well, the whole side seems to respond.

I'm glad somebody decided a long time ago at school that I should be a No. 10.

A lot of fly-halves will tell you that they detest playing against flankers who have a lot of speed. These fly-halves usually respond to the challenge of the fliers by either passing immediately or kicking – classic examples of passing the buck and limiting options. Personally, I enjoy playing against fliers. The good ones hit you now and then, it's true, but by the very nature of their specialist role they give you a chance. It is possible to beat the flier in a man-for-man situation, and your game and sharpness improve dramatically when you can 'slip' the flier who makes a bee-line for you.

There are a lot of complaints that there aren't many flying flankers around these days. I bemoan the fact, too, but for another reason. Most contemporary flankers are much of a muchness and they are the bane of fly-half play because they compensate for their lack of speed by spreading across the field, shadowing rather than trying for an immediate tackle. This not only limits a fly-half's options but often forces him to run flat with the result that the midfield becomes cramped and congested. Some of the best and fastest wings in the world have found themselves ambushed by defences just because a relatively slow opposition flanker has run threateningly and laterally at the fly-half. These flankers who stand off are very difficult to beat with a break.

It seems to me that generally these days there is much too much emphasis on defence. Many players at the top level, particularly backs, are picked principally because of their defensive capabilities, their ability to tackle counting for more than their ability to get their line moving smoothly, to kick or pass well, or to make a break. It is of genuine regret to me that in a game whose popularity and enjoyment has always been based upon flair and spontaneity, a missed tackle has become the most heinous crime on the rugby field, and that one of the consequences of this is the creation of a negative approach among players which is alien to most of them. Players thus reproached not only become terrified of missing a tackle, but they become ultra-cautious in all other aspects of their play.

As a result we have dull, boring and entirely predictable action in most games at the top level. Whatever happened to the old maxim that attack is the best form of defence?

In my own small way, I have tried to play a balanced game, consistent with sensible defence but mindful that one's whole approach can be smothered by a safety-first attitude. I'm an angry old man, though, when I see fine young players with enormous potential for attack being inhibited by defensive requirements. Looking back over my career, I cannot think of one defensive fly-half who has given me trouble, or one who has limited my scope. On the contrary, the biggest problems I've had to contend with have usually been presented by fly-halves who *attack* you.

John Rutherford, of Scotland, is a good example. John is a most difficult opponent. Several times in a match, John will take you on, and give you plenty to think about. Early in his international career Rutherford was not the best of kickers; but this aspect of his game has improved and he is now a most formidable opponent, with fine all-round ability. John represents a good contrast with another fly-half, Naas Botha. Naas has a limited fly-half game, and he is one of those rare birds, a player who has reached the top by virtue of his kicking alone. Botha's kicking, though, is extraordinary. With him kicking is a gift.

I was far more impressed with another South African player, Ray Mordt. Ray's immense strength and genuine pace were something to be admired – even by the opposition. No less admirable is that silky runner Steve Pokere, who has the enviable ability to cause consternation to any defence. France play Serge Blanco at full-back, but he has the skill and pace to play anywhere. Serge has a great attitude to the game, which to my mind is his greatest quality. There is a lot of talk today about the athleticism – or lack of it – of forwards. A supreme athletic forward, to my mind, is Gary Whetton, and if New Zealand manage to get together another seven like him, look out world.

When one talks of the gifted players of world rugby, it is impossible to omit Terry Holmes. His strength and commitment have been admired everywhere, but I find it surprising that he has not been given more credit for his basic skills. It is difficult to pinpoint one weakness in his game.

Everybody, of course, has a favourite player. I suppose I could be accused of prejudice in that none of my heroes are fly-halves, but nevertheless I have no hesitation in nominating Gerald Davies as the best equipped player I have seen or played with. Gerald was in a class of his own, a craftsman with a genuine love of the game. Unlike many other 'greats' Gerald never had a bad game and his consistently high standards set him apart, to be revered and, dare I say it, to be imitated.

'You can fool some of the people all of the time,
and all of the people some of the time,
but you cannot fool all of the people all the time'

Abraham Lincoln

11
THE DAY OF THE COACH

When Ieuan Evans' committee produced its report on the state of Welsh rugby in 1985, it embraced every aspect of the game. The report, which took three years to compile, made many laudable recommendations for the improvement of our game. The tenor of the report left no doubt as to the thoroughness with which the committee had set about their task. The seriousness with which they undertook it, and wanted it to be received, was implicit in the language. To express a criticism of such a wide-ranging document might be considered carping, but it seems that the all-important area of the game in Wales, coaching, was dealt with in a relatively perfunctory manner. This could be explained by the fact that three members of the committee were either coaches or coaching advisors, and that they saw no reason to delve too deeply into this aspect of Welsh rugby.

For some time now, I have pondered the extent to which coaching has infiltrated the Welsh rugby mentality, and asked myself whether it has gone too far.

When Wales introduced organised coaching, the world sat up and took notice. Many countries, envious of the system, sent representatives to examine it first-hand. They went away, I'm sure, feeling that Wales had got things right. What they, and a lot of other people, failed to recognise was that the introduction of the coaching system coincided with a golden era in Welsh rugby, and it's possible that too much credence was given to the system in relation to the contribution of the players, some of whom were among the greatest we've ever produced. No-one questioned whether coaching worked or not. They accepted its credibility, its increasing influence. With Wales winning Triple Crowns, Grand Slams and Championships, the system was bound to be right, wasn't it?

Slowly, insidiously, the coaching system infiltrated every nook and cranny of Welsh rugby, from the schoolboy game right through to national level. Like bottle caps in a brewery, coaches were turned out in profusion from the Aberystwyth courses, clutching their diplomas and soon wearing their badges which declared proudly: 'I'm a WRU coach'. If you had the paper and the badge you were a coach. If you did not, you were the subject of reproof or scorn or pity. The Day of the Coach had arrived and, in my view, a once imaginative, flourishing game is now suffering because he has become our dictator, our god.

I'm not blaming the coaches themselves, but the system which produced them. A string of eager, conscientious people, who worked hard to qualify and earn the right to become a coach, have been created. But sadly the system has not been geared to produce men of vision, of innovation, or of daring, but coaches indistinguishable in their sameness: dully methodical, pedantic, disciplined and organised. What they are, and the methods they have adopted, is what the game in Wales has become. We now pray at the altar of set moves, of organised play. The day of the free, impromptu player is over. The decisions are chalked up on a blackboard, and players are terrified of trying something different. The spark, the flair has gone out of Welsh rugby and, more worrying, we are breeding youngsters who know no different. We teach them fitness, press-ups, and set moves, but the system ignores the development of individual skills.

John Bevan, the Wales coach, has tried very hard to give Wales an identity, but he is handicapped by arbitrary thinking. On one hand, John will say: 'I encourage players to do what they want', and the next moment, he will be dismissive: 'you mustn't do this or that'. Doesn't anyone realise that if the only thing you do at squad sessions is to practise over and over again certain set moves, you will do precisely the same thing when it comes to the match? If there is no spontaneity in training, there will be no spontaneity in a match. Set-move orientated players, in reality, are not required to think. Doggedly they repeat what has been drummed into them. The choice, the option, never occurs to them. When a player 'rebels', and says to hell with it, and tries something on his own, and it goes wrong, he is slated by the coach for the indiscretion. You could even find yourself kicked out of the side because you have not conformed. It is a dangerous path we're treading, to give so much power to the coach.

It would be facile to suggest that we should abandon the coaching system altogether. But it certainly needs a thorough overhaul. We need men of vision to get it by the scruff of the neck and shake out the dogma, and rid our game of stereotyped coaching.

I can visualise only one man capable of doing this – John Dawes. Given the right sort of circumstances, John should resign his present job and offer himself as coaching supremo. He must hide his head in embarrassment to stand witness to the sterile rugby being produced in the name of coaching. Would he, a proponent of flair and style, one who encourages natural skills, ask the Welsh team, for instance, to spend the whole of one session – the main one before the match – without the ball, simply defending against the rest of the squad? That's what happened in our preparation for the 1984 Australia match, and it showed the negative approach, the caution, the rigidity, that has pervaded the game.

Someone once suggested to me that the answer to dull, monotonous training sessions was to substitute them with touch rugby, sub-dividing the players into little groups of five players. He could have a point. At least we would get back to situations in which the emphasis is on skill, positioning, reaction, on quick, accurate passing, on beating a man. That's what rugby is all about, surely. Maybe touch rugby is not as daft as it may appear.

Little of the foregoing represents new argument or fresh thought. Most of it has occupied my mind for many years now, and it is perhaps interesting to reflect that my ideas have not radically altered for several years. As long ago as 1981 I was invited, as a player, to give a talk to a WRU coaching conference at the Cardiff Sports Centre. The following is the gist of that talk – the reader can guess for himself the reaction, and judge whether a player's view was taken seriously:

'I don't know if I should thank anyone for asking me here today to give a talk to all you gentlemen who have devoted most of your spare time to this great game of rugby. I am a little apprehensive about that. If I should say something with which you don't agree, I'm sure it will be discussed in future sessions.

'John Dawes invited me, and gave me full scope to talk on any subject. I presume he meant me to confine myself to the game, and not other matters, such as the social events of Cardiff's recent trip to Zimbabwe. I shall try to do exactly that – though I must say that these are largely spontaneous thoughts. They may sound like criticisms as probably you have all spent the weekend praising your own coaching systems.

'"Wales – a nation spoiled by success". This is a recent saying, and sums up the situation we as a rugby country find ourselves in today. After a decade at the pinnacle of European rugby, we now find ourselves in the middle of the pack, so to speak, as far as results are concerned, bracketed with England. It is a situation which all of us in the current Welsh squad very much regret.

'The past ten years, that golden era, coincided as we all know with the appearance on the playing fields of the world of probably some of the greatest players of all time – players like Barry John, Gareth Edwards, Mervyn Davies, J.P.R. and Gerald Davies. This forces me to ask: is it purely coincidence that these great players grew up and learned their rugby before the advent of coaching? Did they grasp the basic skills at an early age purely by natural instinct and then, as they matured, did coaching smooth off the rough edges and make them appreciate that they were only part of a team and that they had to conform and serve as links in that team, and not just perform as individuals? It's important to note that these players learned their trade instinctively.

'Where has coaching taken us now? Let us look at one side of it, the worst in my view. A year or so ago, I was watching a schoolboy trial in the Pontypridd area, when my attention was diverted to an adjoining pitch where a group of under 11s was being supervised by their "coach" – and I emphasise coach in inverted commas. I stood amazed as these young lads of ten years old – the internationals of tomorrow – were ordered to do press-ups, sit-ups, piggy backs etc. I couldn't help comparing that with things in my day – I don't think I ever did a press-up until I went on a coaching course at Aberystwyth when I was 16 or 17. Perhaps that's the reason why I'm not the greatest crash tackler in Wales! But seriously, if what happened at Pontypridd is an example of what WRU coaches are instructed to do, then I think we are heading the wrong way.

'Thinking back a few years, I recall some members of the 1977 Lions tour of New Zealand telling "horror" stories of how they had watched boys of six and seven playing competitive rugby in New Zealand, with their parents and, of course, coaches on the touch-line baying for blood and success. If we are honest with ourselves, that's exactly what's happening here now. We are in the same position, with far too much competitive rugby organised at too early an age. Coaches and parents are hungry for success, not only for the children, tomorrow's players, but also in a way to benefit themselves from a kind of reflected glory. I've been coached now for ten years and I find it's getting more difficult to enjoy training. Imagine what these young lads will feel like when they get to their early twenties. There is a great danger that they will become disillusioned with the game, and we might lose them altogether. You can hardly blame them.

'I would also like to make a few comments about that word "success". Today there is so much pressure on players to win matches and be successful that we have all become victims of the system, with no-one wanting to know you if you are a loser. You have to look no further than our own WRU Cup, a very popular tournament in most respects. I'm not criticising the competition, as I thoroughly enjoy it and it has certainly aroused a great response in interest. But if we look back at nearly all the finals that have been played, hardly one stands out in terms of quality. We, in Cardiff, can look back at this year's final [1981] and think to ourselves, what a great day. But that was only about being successful, and all that John Scott, myself and John Ryan, our coach, were interested in. But ask yourself, what of the quality of the play? As players today, we are coached to win. It is sad that the system doesn't allow us to enjoy ourselves if we lose. When we do lose, we are attacked by the coach and the selectors for, say, being too loose, or missing tackles. Is it fair that players are dropped because of this? We mustn't forget the media in all this. Inevitably they have their stab at the losers, and can easily damage a player's confidence.

'Today's coaching I feel is perhaps negative in the sense that it is geared to eliminating errors and does not try to promote imaginative play – not only among the backs but also the forwards. The forwards, after all, are not on the field just to scrummage with their backsides in the air, they are there to *play* rugby. This negative approach has infected the players themselves. We find ourselves discussing other players – "he's no good as a flanker, he can only run". Daft, isn't it? What's wrong with that? The game is about running with the ball and here we are panning someone because that's what he does.

'I hope I can appreciate the coach's problem. He is judged as a good or bad coach by his team's results, which brings us back again to winning being all important. Take for example Australia's attitude only this week – they promised a new approach to the game when they beat New Zealand last year, but because they were so desperate to beat France, they decided to abandon their method to put safety first and dropped their most exciting ball-handler, Mark Ella, simply because he didn't fit into the coach's idea of a winning side.

'Talking of Ella, one of the best handlers and passers of a ball that I've seen, leads me on to passing. In my view, not enough emphasis is placed on orthodox passing in coaching sessions. As players we are all guilty today of wanting to do fancy moves and practise these moves in training. How many players can take and give a pass in one movement – not many I'm afraid. Even the general standard of passing is not high. I feel we should concentrate more on simple, orthodox passing and passing under pressure. Boring? On the contrary. One of the most enjoyable sessions I've had in recent years was with John Dawes in Australia in 1978 when we practised passing for an hour, trying to achieve objectives. I feel that passing properly has got to be initiated at school level so that by the time the youngsters mature, the giving and taking of a pass is second nature to them. It's very difficult to teach a person of, say, 25 to do this; and today's senior players are now so used to practising moves that some would just laugh off the idea of a session of orthodox passing.

'Another point concerning training, especially for backs, is that we don't play enough touch rugby or some similar game in which we could use skills to beat men, or improve our other skills with the ball, whether it be by hand or foot. You hear of complaints that today's players don't take on opponents enough, in other words do not try to beat them by flair. My answer to that is that practice makes perfect and we don't get much practice at it. The only opportunity we get is in the match itself on a Saturday afternoon.

'Perhaps back play generally has suffered over the last few years because of the increased concentration on forward techniques, especially scrummaging. To me, a mere back, surely a scrum is just a way to re-start a match after an infringement, but few coaches place a strong emphasis on this aspect. Where have all the quick balls gone from the scrums? This is a sign of loose or carefree play, which inevitably means slow ball for the backs, and as a result, the attacking side have tended to create second-phase play.

'What about more emphasis on scoring tries? Remember the Floodlit Alliance in which the game was about tries, not kicks? They threw that out because of the increased burden on players. What has happened since? Instead of the Floodlit Alliance, we now have floodlit mid-week matches, which are a major part of every club's fixture programme. Why not use these mid-week matches to try to promote running rugby in which the scoring of tries is the main purpose of the exercise? These are only a few points, but I hope I have conveyed to you the feelings of today's players.'

When you discuss how the game is played you cannot, of course, leave out referees and the laws. You hear plenty of complaints that players are no longer enjoying the game, but I've come to the inescapable conclusion that neither are referees. Where once there was a smile and a quip from them, we now seem to have a sullen grimace and short, sharp remarks like 'get on with the game'.

Part of the problem may stem from the perpetual tinkering with the laws by the lawmakers, and referees are finding it increasingly difficult to administer the changes with uniformity. Interpretation – or the lack of it – has become a byword for fierce argument, both on and off the field, and referees seem to be under greater scrutiny and pressure than they have ever been. I'm now convinced that referees are beginning to exert far too much influence on play, and they seem to me to be more concerned with their own performance, as seen by outside observers, than with the effect their new hard-line approach to the laws is having on players and the game. Pedantry over the laws is now common, and it is making the game very difficult.

A case in point was Cardiff's match against the Fijians in 1985, which was refereed by Winston Jones – someone, incidentally, I have known since I was a schoolboy. Whether there was someone in the stands watching or assessing Winston I do not know, but the way he applied the laws in this match really concerned me, particularly with regard to the ruck. In fact, we did not have one genuine ruck in the match. Once the ball was on the floor, it seemed that Winston would blow up and call for a scrum. This attitude was a common factor in most matches in Wales at the start of the 1985 season, and I believe the increasing complaints from the forwards emphasise a real concern that perhaps our referees are going to blow the ruck out of existence in the United Kingdom. The Canterbury versus Auckland match, which I watched on television the day after Cardiff played the Fijians showed that in New Zealand they have a different approach to rucking, or at least their referees are not hell-bent on eliminating that feature of the game. The new laws, which came into operation at the start of the Northern

Hemisphere season in September 1985, are clearly looked at differently in the Southern Hemisphere where they were in operation for six months before our referees were required to put them into practice. When I say 'our', I mean of course, British referees. Needless to say, the new laws are interpreted differently in England than they are in Wales, and when David Matthews, of Liverpool, handled the Swansea versus Llanelli match on same day that Cardiff played the Fijians, the players were up in arms, often at a loss at some of his decisions, particularly with regard to ruck and tackle. Referees, it seems, are so intent on stringently applying the laws in that respect that they are even overlooking any possibility of allowing advantage.

Referees also seem to be nit-picking in the line-out: even a slight deviation in the line-out throw is reason for another blast on the whistle, another scrum. Only one referee I know, Derek Bevan, has a good attitude to the line-out. He lets most trivial things go, realising as all players do that everything balances out in the end, and that neither side is at a disadvantage if, for instance, the throw-in is occasionally crooked.

I suspect that the reason for this new dour approach is that the authorities are demanding more of our referees. The referees are put under a lot of pressure these days, and that pressure is being transferred through the play to the players. The only referee, it seems to me, who has remained unaffected and who still laughs and jokes on the field, and discusses incidents with players, is Clive Norling. The game fortunately has not become too intense or serious for him, and although as a player you might argue with some of his decisions, he is highly respected for his attitude and his fairness. Certainly players do not get the impression with Clive as they do with other referees that he is playing to an audience, looking to impress others. If he is a bit of a showman, that is hardly a fault in a game in which characters are becoming fewer and fewer.

Quite a number of good referees, some very popular with players, have quit in recent years, stating that they no longer enjoy the game. This is a pity, for while I appreciate their difficulties, I'm sure they would have lasted a little longer if they had allowed their own personalities to come through and had said to hell with what others think of them. Rapport between players and referees is much more important than people realise.

'For it's a way we have in the Baa-Baas,
And a jolly good way too,
For it's a way we have in the Baa-Baas,
And a rule that we play to;
For the rugby game, we do not train
We play it with a will
For it's a way we have in the Baa-Baas
And a jolly good way too!'

Barbarian FC club song

12
THE BARBARIANS

When I received a letter in the summer of 1985 from Herbert Waddell, president of the Barbarians, inviting me to become a committee man with the club, I suspected at once that this was no sinecure, and that some proof would be required that I had the qualities needed to be a Baa-Baa alickadoo. I considered the matter gravely. By the time I had sent off my grateful acceptance to Herbert, I was reasonably confident that I was equal to any test that might be forthcoming. What was needed, obviously, was a list of requirements for being a competent Barbarian committee man. I tore up the original draft (too long), and the next (pathetically short), and ultimately decided on a master list. Clearly the first priority would be to undertake a crash course in elocution – I'd need the confidence to beg, borrow or steal a street map of Cardiff, an identity-tag engraved c/o the Royal Hotel (finder will be rewarded), a silver hip flask, a tartan rug, a Harris tweed suit, a Cambridge Blue mohair waistcoat, an Oxford Blue Crombie top coat, a forged letter stating that my golf handicap was 18, a copy (also forged) of an application for membership of the East India & Sports Club, and lastly a paperback of *Finding Fossils* by F.F. Fosdyke and/or the RFU Handbook. Apart from withdrawal symptoms, I decided there would be little hardship in allowing myself a month or so to prepare for the constitutional shock of switching from Brain's Dark to pink gin, malt whisky and champagne.

I sent my master list to Jeff Herdman, the Swansea coach, knowing that he too had received a like invitation from Mr Waddell, and was stepping up his training in preparation for the change from player to committee man. Jeff's reply, posted with a second class stamp, took only ten days to get to me, but in general terms he approved of my list although he was concerned that perhaps I'd overlooked some of the requirements. What about a red carnation buttonhole, he asked, and gold-rimmed pince-nez specs, an ivory handled Malacca-cane shooting-stick and a deerstalker? You have to be firm with hookers, so I told him straight: No, I said, they'd be just a wee bit ostentatious even for a Barbarian alickadoo. Must try to avoid drawing attention to yourself, mustn't you?

Of course, I may have gone to all this trouble for nothing. It's possible that like a lot of people in the game, I've gained an entirely wrong impression of the Baa-Baa alickadoo, and that the notion that he is odd, reactionary, stuffy and blimpish is based either on prejudice, envy or myopia, or a mixture of all three. I realise why. The Baa-Baas are a coy bunch; they rarely present themselves for public scrutiny, do not divulge their business or their way of doing it, and they rely entirely for their corporate image on what takes place on the field of play. It occurs to me that those are the credentials for the perfect rugby club, and if the shadowy, remote people who administer its affairs never step forward into the glare of the spotlight, it is because they have no need to do so. The *raison d'être* of the Barbarians is to invite players who enjoy playing to compete against quality opposition, and in the process to provide a rare opportunity for them to measure their ability against some of the best players in the world. If the Baa-Baas are regarded as anachronistic, it is only because they've always done things in this way, and no-one has yet come up with a reason to make any changes.

The problem is that alickadoos are not immortal. Some die or merely fade away or get their telephones cut off. So from time to time the Barbarian officials have to look around for replacements for the committee. New blood you might say. That their two latest acquisitions, Jeff and myself, are still actively playing is an unusual departure for the Baa-Baas, who normally make their choice from older, long retired players. I suspect their motive in roping in Jeff and I is a feeling that we are close to the playing scene, and might have some 'pull' in inducing players to turn out for the club.

The selection of players is a bigger problem than it might first appear. Every player, you'd think, would give an arm or a leg to play for the Barbarians. To be a member of a team in which every player is of the highest calibre is a challenge, an honour comparable with playing for your country or touring with the Lions. But wanting to play, and being able to are two different matters. The Baa-Baas have found in recent years a measure of reluctance on the part of players to accept their invitations, not because they do not wish to play, but because of conflicting loyalties, the priority usually being club commitments, tours and the like. The Barbarians could of course play a nondescript side, but to do that would be to fall short of their own high standards, and would hardly please the opposition clubs, most of whom regard the Barbarian match as a plum fixture. Players are also playing a great deal more often than they used to. I'll bet Geoff Windsor-Lewis, the Baa-Baas secretary, has lost count of the number of times, for instance, that a player who has agreed to play has had to withdraw late in the day because he has been injured in the interim. Replacing that injured player at short notice has become a real headache. I had first-hand experience of it when Windsor-Lewis, tapping his new source, as it were, approached me for suggestions for a replacement to join the Barbarian team to play London Welsh at Twickenham in September 1985, two days before the game was due to be played. A lot of telephoning and hustling around failed to provide a solution, but fortunately even though I failed (largely because of the obstacle of club commitments) another Baa-Baa 'scout' saved the day.

Despite the difficulties, I'm certain the Barbarians will continue to prosper. They have a unique and important place in rugby, and even though the game is undergoing rapid and major changes, they are an institution which must be preserved because fundamentally the club exists for players and for their enjoyment.

My first contact with the club was at Easter in 1975, when they came to the Arms Park to play their annual match against

Cardiff. We saw them off, five tries to two with a 24-19 result. It is unusual in any match for both half-backs to score a try, but Brynmor Williams and myself managed one apiece. The biggest Arms Park cheer, however, was reserved for Ian Robinson's try, his second against the Baa-Baas for he had scored in the equivalent match in 1972.

I played against the Baa-Baas again in 1976, that extraordinary match when we recovered from the dead, 0-24 down, to pip them 29-28. No try this time, but three conversions helped, although the real hero was Gareth Edwards with his match-winning dropped goal. The Baa-Baas captain that day was Ian McGeechan, and when he pulled out of their tour to Canada and the USA later in the year, I got my unexpected chance to wear that famous jersey. We played two matches as part of the Boston Bicentennial Tournament and six matches in Canada. An indication of the type of rugby we played (and of the standard of the opposition) was a total of 76 tries from the eight matches, including 16 in one of them. The 76-0 defeats of Saskatchewan and of Atlantic All Stars remain the highest score achieved by any Barbarian side. As I have related elsewhere, I had the personal satisfaction of scoring 31 points, my highest total in a match, against Quebec.

At the start of the following season (September 1976) I was part of the Barbarian team invited to play in Cardiff's Centenary Sevens, and although we lost in the final, to Newport, I took some delight in scoring three tries against Cardiff in the semi-final. The Baa-Baas are always warmly welcomed by the Arms Park crowd, but I'm not sure what they thought of my role in helping to knock out my own club.

Thereafter I played regularly for the Baa-Baas against Leicester, but the match I best remember was one that didn't take place. I was vice-captain against Australia in 1982, but the finale of their tour was cancelled because of heavy snow. Instead we settled ourselves in for a great day on the Friday, in the Royal Hotel, and we certainly had one. I got the last taxi to run out of Cardiff that night, but Dai Richards was stranded for two days or more before he found his way back to Swansea through the snowdrifts.

Not the least of the attractions of being a Baa-Baa player is the social side. It gives you an opportunity of meeting and conversing with players you rarely meet, because when the Baa-Baas cast their net, it is a wide one. They 'import' Irish lads and Frenchmen, as well as the usual quota of Englishmen, Scots and Welsh. The ambience of a Baa-Baas get-together is remarkable considering the often widely different views and habitats of the members. You learn a lot, without seeking to. Someone will tell you of the exploits of a Paddy twice as big as Moss Keane, another of a rave-up at Hawick, or of expenses showering like confetti in a certain French club, or of a Welshman trying to introduce line-out signals in Welsh at Aitch-Kew. Such gossip flows freely and naturally in a good atmosphere, and I'm sure it helps the *esprit de corps.* Refreshments help as well. When I was appointed captain against Australia in 1984, I was given a fairly free hand with both the training and the entertainment. One we took lightly, the other seriously. A visit to the Horse and Groom pub in Cardiff seemed a good idea at the time, until one of the lads inquired if I was paying. No, I replied, I was kitty-less. It was a fraught situation, but fortunately the day was saved when the landlord agreed to run up a slate. Good for team spirit, I kept repeating to myself as we walked back to our hotel later with a bill for £65. I presented it to Gordon Ferguson, the Baa-Baas' assistant secretary. 'Fergie' took one look at it, nodded, and proceeded to write out a cheque. There are no quibbles either the day after we play. There's always a champagne breakfast before the players disband, which strikes me as a nice final touch, something which players appreciate and of course remember.

The 1984 match against the Aussies was special in other ways. In the first place, the Baa-Baas don't have a coaching session as such, in fact they haven't even got a coach. The preparation is usually left to the captain. In this case, the captain had a good plan: let the lads get on with it. We had two blithe sessions of half an hour each, and it was a joy to take part in them, admiring the exuberance of Spikey Watkins, the pace of Serge Blanco, the smooth acceleration of Rory Underwood and the snap passes of Jerome Gallion. Light-hearted or not that team, with all its differences and makeshift appearance, had a tremendous spirit. They really wanted to play, really wanted to beat the Australians – and they very nearly did. It is impossible not to compare our almost frivolous build-up with the tense, serious and dour preparation employed by Wales against Australia earlier in the tour. I'm not suggesting Wales bring in Les Dawson to run things, but I'm sure a happy, unpressured team is more likely to perform better than one that is not.

When I look back over my long association with the Barbarians, I realise that the fun element, off the field as well as on it, meant a great deal to me. One of the most enduring memories, however, is only indirectly associated with the club, but whenever I recall it, I allow myself a little private chuckle.

I was guesting, along with Willie Carson, the jockey, in Bill Beaumont's team in *Question of Sport* on BBC TV in 1982 when David Coleman, the question-master, offered me my 'home' question, on rugby. 'Which club was formed in Yorkshire over an oyster supper, has no pitch of its own, and whose last overseas tour was in 1969?' Bill smiled, absolutely confident that I knew. 'I'm sorry, I've no idea', I said. David, a little disdainfully I thought, told me: 'The Barbarians, of course'. I hesitated, considered the matter for a moment and said: 'Excuse me David. I think that's wrong. I was on the last Baa-Baas tour to Canada – in 1976'. David looked as if he was going to explode. 'What the f...'s going on?' he blurted out, in front of a studio audience of 200. Fortunately for all concerned, including the person who set the question, the programme was recorded, and millions of TV viewers missed the *faux pas.* The question, and David's response, were edited out.

'I look upon the world as my parish'

John Wesley

13
A TRAVELLER'S TALE

Touring means different things to different people, but in an amateur sport it is still the only tangible reward for a player. With the world continuing to shrink in terms of accessibility, you don't have to be a prophet to forsee that the appeal of packing your kit and setting off for faraway fields and exotic locations will continue to increase.

The tour bug bit me in 1976 when I accompanied the Barbarians to Canada. Someone only had to mention 'tour' to me thereafter and I was flourishing my passport. There are all sorts of tours, some on which the rugby is a serious component, and others where playing is incidental. It makes no difference to me. Long or short, sensible or booze cruises, I'm addicted. There are several reasons for the obsession. Most important, I suppose, is that I always play my best rugby on tour. Playing-wise, I've never had a bad tour, although I've had a few set-backs, like being injured on the 1980 British Lions tour to South Africa. Tour ambience is vital to someone like me, a socialiser. Away, I'm what John Scott describes as laid back. I let the whole thing wash over me like a deliciously warm Caribbean sea. The relaxed, easy-going atmosphere, good food and hospitality does marvellous things for my constitution after a cold, damp Welsh winter.

The best part of touring for me, especially on a serious tour, is après-match. W.G.D. is in his element when the tour group hold a private get-together for an hour or so at the hotel. The jokes, the horseplay and the singing seem to unite the team, to build the camaraderie and to cement friendships. Nothing equals the team party, and I get quite emotional whenever I look back over the dozens that I've been involved in over the years. Although they all contained the same elements, none were ever exactly alike. Most are successful because of their spontaneity, yet probably they would not work without a script.

Cardiff, for example, always respond to an MC, such as Scottie or the irrepressible Spikey Watkins, when he was with us. The MC's job is to evaluate how the party is going, to anticipate lulls, to drum up the action. Usually this means a contribution from anyone the MC cares to nominate – the good, the bad and the ugly. My party piece rarely varied outside dreadful renderings of Christopher Robin and Winnie the Pooh, the Leaving of Liverpool, or a Welsh hymn. No matter how bad, you're always required to do your bit. Holmesy's specialities were Showaddywaddy hits, and Pablo (Paul) Rees did The Ugly Bug Ball and Running Bear. Contender for top Cardiff performer was however Ian Robinson. No matter how often we heard his contribution, it always brought roars of approval:

> 'I am Ian Robinson
> I am big and strong
> I used to play for Wales
> but not for f...ing long'

I was an innocent abroad on that first tour with the Barbarians. When I was called into the squad after Ian McGeechan had pulled out, I had to obtain special leave from UWIST, who agreed to postpone my second year exams. Naïvely I decided I would take some books with me for revision. Work? It was a joke. I don't think I even opened a book the whole time I was there. You learn other things, as you cautiously try to keep up with everyone. It was like tip-toeing through a minefield. You never knew what was going to happen next. I was not too worried about tour rule number one – 'no sleeping on tour' – but as a newcomer, the baby of the tour, I soon realised I was a sitting duck for the Machiavellian pranks of the seasoned tourers. First lesson was 'trust no-one'. After a 'beer bash' in a lift in a big hotel in Montreal, which was novel to say the least, I must have missed the winks. Before I knew what was happening a few of the lads, led by Gareth Jenkins, the former Llanelli flanker, decided I was overdressed. By the time the lift opened in the foyer on the ground floor I was wearing nothing but a simpering smile.

Did I allow this to put me off Montreal? Certainly not. I had one of the best matches of my life there, against Quebec. I scored two tries, a penalty and ten conversions – 31 points – which was not only my best-ever score in a match but, I believe, a record by a Barbarian. I thought Wales could have few equals when it came to picturesque countryside until I went to Canada. I was staggered by its beauty, its wildness, the sheer overwhelming size of the place. Seeing Niagara Falls for the first time was breathtaking for a youngster who, at the time, considered Devil's Bridge Falls one of the wonders of the world.

I liked the USA too, on the same tour. We stayed at Boston College, next to Harvard University in size. The facilities there seemed astounding to me. The college had a 50,000-seater stadium, astroturf and three tartan tracks, one of them indoor. At the time there were only two or three tartan tracks in the whole of the United Kingdom.

Going to Australia with Wales in 1978 was an altogether different experience. Rugby took pride of place, which was understandable as it was there that I gained my first caps. Being first choice fly-half for the whole tour curtailed the social side: early to bed, diligent training and all that. I didn't mind. I realised a lot was expected of the players, and not one of us was unwilling to sacrifice something to do well on the field. Sadly, things did not work out well in that respect, and I think even some of the battle-hardened Welsh forwards were surprised by the cynical, physical approach of the Australians in the Tests. Graham Price had his jaw broken in the Second Test at Sydney, but the first match at Ballymore was much dirtier. After one ruck, which Australia won, I looked around to see how our defence was lined up to cope and was mildly surprised that no-one was there. Gravs, Fenwick and J.J. were all involved in fisticuffs on the other side of the field. As Australia launched a 4-1 overlap in my direction, I must admit the whole thing seemed absurd, so unnecessary. Is this what international rugby is all about, I asked myself. Some of the more mature players did a good job in shrugging off the dirty play aspect and Wales' defeats. I found it impossible to bottle up my emotions. After the Second Test, I cried in the changing-rooms.

I have toured South Africa five times, the first with Cardiff in 1979, which was a good tour in most respects, even though I arrived there with my leg in plaster because of an ankle injury. The standard of rugby in South Africa is always tremendously high and only the most dedicated tourists have a chance of pulling off good results. Cardiff played well generally, and it was an excellent performance to beat Natal in our last match. When a top side goes there, acres of space are given over to the tour in the newspapers. Players are featured in every possible way, and when they don't have a story to write they invent one. It was in South Africa that I was described as the 'Bobby Ewing lookalike', a trifle to my discomfiture, but to the approval of the rest of the Cardiff team, heedful of an alternative to my then current nickname, Majid, which originated because (they said) I looked more Pakistani than Welsh. At least that newspaper got one thing right: 'Bobby'll be back next year with the Lions', it predicted.

A Lions tour is very important to the South Africans, as we discovered in 1980. Getting off the plane at Jan Smuts Airport in Johannesburg we were greeted by thousands. It was an incredible sight. And I thought the Welsh were rugby-mad!

That tour will always be known as the injury-jinxed one, and the fact that the Lions were forced to send an SOS for seven replacements disguised a much longer casualty list. From the first minute of the first match, when Stuart Lane was ruled out, through to the end, the Lions went down like ninepins, and regardless of the arguments about tactics and ill-luck in the Tests, this catastrophic injury problem was the fundamental explanation for our defeat in the series. My own injury jinx also struck in that first match, against Eastern Province at Port

Elizabeth. It could not have been more infuriating, because not only was I spanking fit, but I had got off to a great start. You're always looking to boost your own confidence and everything was working out perfectly for me with a penalty, a dropped goal and a break from a line-out which led to Mike Slemen racing over. I'd given the pass when a slightly late crash tackle put my shoulder out, and although I stayed on to kick the conversion, I was bitterly disappointed to have to join Stuart on the injury bench. Stuart never played again, and flew home. I was out for two weeks, which was frustratingly long, because with Ollie Campbell also unfit, the Lions had a major problem at fly-half which was only partly solved by Tony Ward joining us.

Ollie and I stayed in Johannesburg for treatment. Clive Noble, a doctor with unequalled knowledge of sports injuries, ministered to us marvellously at his clinic. Eventually he prescribed a cortisone injection for me. It was my first experience of cortisone, although I'd heard whispers that the thought of receiving it had made braver men than me whimper. I knew what I was in for when Dr Noble called for an assistant to hold me down. Dr Noble was a real character, and thorough. He wanted to find out first-hand the kind of pain some of his patients endured. On the day of the First Test, he ran in the Comrades Marathon, from Pietersmaritsburg to Durban, which was a small matter of 54 miles. I think we can describe that as dedication beyond the call of duty.

I was not fit for that First Test and although Tony Ward scored 18 points, a couple of loose punts led to the Springboks scoring tries and winning. I was declared fit for the next match, against a coloured side at Windhoek, and although I was not 100 per cent I eased my way through. W.G.D. was back on the tour road, and I was over the moon, as our footballing brethren describe high elation. Rave reports in the Press followed our next match, against Transvaal, when Colin Patterson, Clive Woodward and myself 'hit it off'. The omens could not have been brighter for the Second Test, only for Dai Richards, and then Terry Holmes, to join the injured list. The series probably hung on that Second Test, at Bloemfontein.

The 'Boks were 16-15 ahead but the Lions were beginning to take control, and I was absolutely confident we'd win. Then disaster struck. I was hit by a high tackle from Naas 'Nasty' Botha, my knee gave way and my tour was over. My left knee ligaments were torn and I was a sorry sight, utterly dispirited with my ill-luck as much as with the Lions' second defeat. One doctor examined me and recommended an immediate operation. Fortunately Clive Noble gave a second opinion. I could ignore an operation but I had to put in a lot of hard work to rebuild the leg. Clive said I'd be out for six months. I was.

There has been a lot of gossip about the Lions' behaviour on the night of the Bloemfontein defeat, and very little of it was based on fact. Certainly, many of us were hell-bent on drowning our sorrows – and some of us had every justification. But nothing got out of hand, at least not until late on, as we were retiring to our rooms. Some South African supporters, not content that their side had won, began to niggle and sneer at a group of us. Someone's parentage was questioned, a drunk lashed out in my direction with a boot only for my 'minder', that tough bruiser Peter Morgan, to crack him with a lovely right hand. Thanks, Pete, I'll do the same for you some time – we big boys have got to stick together.

The next day brought an emotional farewell. The whole tour party was on parade to wish *bon voyage* to the four of us for whom the tour was over; Holmesy, Dai Richards, Fran Cotton and myself. Some of the lads cracked pathetic little jokes, others just stood there not knowing what to do or say. Ray Gravell broke down in tears in the hotel foyer. We thought about them all on that flight home, and we must have toasted each and every one of them in champagne by the time our Jumbo touched down at Heathrow. We were certainly in a better mood than our waiting wives might have expected as we emerged from Customs bright-eyed and just a weeny bit tipsy. No stricken heroes us.

I have been back to South Africa on three other occasions and have established some lasting friendships. I have played with and against South Africans because I like their country and admire the way they play but above all because I have the freedom of choice. Like many players, I find much in their political system abhorrent, but I saw no reason to allow my personal opinions to influence my views as a sportsman. If I were a politician, and thank the Lord I'm not, perhaps I'd have adopted a different stance. It may sound trite, but I believe the world of sport is a far better place when we are allowed to get on with things in our own way without political pressures and interference. If the South Africans make fundamental changes in their political system, which I hope they do, then perhaps rugby players will cease to be brought into issues not of their making.

Cardiff enjoyed participating in a club tournament at Loftus Versfeldt, Pretoria, in 1982, and I went back again later in the year to play for Syd Millar's European XV against Natal and Western Province. In 1983 I was privileged to be included in a World XV which took part in Western Province's centenary. That was a great experience, not least because it was an opportunity to play alongside players of the calibre of Pokere, Shaw, Ashworth and others. It was also quite a challenge to play against South Africa at Newlands – at centre. The South Africans have a munificent attitude when it comes to the treatment of players; they regard it as your right that you are put up at the best hotels, that you get the best kit, blazers etc and that expenses are liberal. The New Zealanders are not as bashful as home countries players when it comes to the delicate question of expenses. 'Any more cabbage today?' was a frequent question from them. They only asked of course because they knew that they would not embarrass the organisers, who usually have access to ample funds. The game in South Africa is a lot healthier, and wealthier, than many realise.

I was invited to join the Crawshay's tour of South Africa in the summer of 1985 when Kevin Thomas was injured at the start of the tour. I said 'no', pleading that I could not spare the time from work. The tour had been arranged earlier in the year and it was unfortunate that the departure of the team coincided with a dramatic, highly publicised increase in the disturbances in South Africa. While supporting Crawshay's' right and decision to tour, I could appreciate some of the arguments against their going, particularly as people were being killed elsewhere in the country at the same time as they were playing. Against this explosive backdrop, perhaps Crawshay's would have been viewed in a better light if they had cancelled the trip. History will judge them in that respect.

Gareth Edwards told me once that if ever I had an opportunity to tour Zimbabwe, I should grab it with both hands, because his experience of playing there put the country high on his list of favourite tours. 'Beautiful', said Gareth, 'Really beautiful.' When Cardiff decided to tour Zimbabwe, I remembered Gareth's enthusiasm. But after four years of non-stop rugby, plus trouble with a nagging knee injury, I was less than eager. In fact, I decided at first I would not go. As the time for finalising arrangements approached, however, and as I had been asked to captain the team, I had a change of heart. I'm glad I did. It was one of the most enjoyable tours I've ever been part of. Cardiff had to face a few ticklish political problems because three of the team – Holmesy, Alan Phillips and myself – had played in South Africa, but once assurances were given in this regard, we were on our way.

The hospitality and welcome we were given were tremendous, and were the same whether we were staying at bustling Salisbury or the lovely country town of Gwelo. Whatever the special interests of individuals – golf, sight-seeing, fishing or horse riding – someone would miraculously appear to lay on the appropriate entertainment. It was organisation *par excellence.* The amazing Victoria Falls, active days at Troutbeck, high in the Inyanga Mountains, and a booze cruise up the Zambesi river rated high in the popularity stakes. Some German tourists were also on the Zambesi boat trip, and were suitably impressed with our choral efforts. Who said we Welsh weren't good ambassadors? On the field, too, Cardiff enjoyed themselves. We were unbeaten, and we played some good sides. I was impressed with the straight running and speed of some of the centres who played against us, and I was personally rather relieved that our forwards had the edge in loose play, because it gave us an advantage in every match.

The South African 'connection' again reared its ugly head

in 1984 when Cardiff were all but on the plane to tour Barbados. Frankly, everybody at the club was heartily sick of the political interference and the tour's cancellation. But in a miracle of rapid reorganisation we switched plans, and direction, and headed instead for Thailand. Fred Rumsey burned a lot of midnight oil in fixing up the tour, but we still gibe him for the erratic flight plan – by Pakistan Airlines via Damascus, Frankfurt, Amsterdam, Karachi and finally Bangkok. I'm still not certain of that itinerary. We stayed overnight in Karachi and 'Majid' had some difficulty in persuading the rest of the team that he really didn't know the fleshpots of the city, and that his knowledge of the language was not exactly native. Thailand was extraordinary in its diversity, and everyone had his own story to tell of visits to Pat Pong, the red light district of Bangkok, of the range of facilities at the Royal Bangkok Sporting Club, of transvestites and others at Pattaya Beach, of golf with hangovers at six in the morning, of Thai boxing . . . it was endless, stimulating variety. I'd go again, but only if assured that the flight was a little more direct.

Another outpost in the growing empire of rugby is the Cayman Islands. I nearly missed a trip there because frankly I had no idea where the islands were. One cold, January morning in 1984, I answered the telephone. Did I want to speak at a dinner, I was asked. My initial lack of enthusiasm showed as I dithered. Only when the caller, John Rees, explained that the function was the Cayman Islands RFC annual dinner, and that they were prepared to fly me and Helen there, was my enthusiasm kindled. Yes, I said, I'd speak – and I hadn't a clue where in this big, beautiful world of ours the Cayman Islands were. The dinner could have been held in Robinson Crusoe's hut and Man Friday could have been the chef for all I knew about Cayman Islands RFC. But then, that's the fun part of going abroad: the adventure, the discoveries, the surprises.

Roughly speaking, the Caymans are near the West Indies, and to get there meant a flight via Miami and over-flying Cuba to Grand Cayman, the largest island in the group. Helen hasn't had many opportunities to accompany me on rugby trips, and obviously she was looking forward to it, probably more than I was, because after-dinner speaking isn't exactly my idea of a fun night out. Still, we'd said yes, and we were on our way, with something of the anticipation and excitement of a second honeymoon. We could not have found a more perfect spot for such sentimentality. We were welcomed at Georgetown airport by Barry Smith, who, with his wife Ann, was to be our kind host for ten days at their luxurious beachside apartment. It was fabulous, a fairytale place with the warm, blue sea lapping just feet away from the patio, and the balmy, Mediterranean-type climate made our stay even more satisfying. Helen adored it, and would have been more than willing to stay forever. She was genuinely disappointed when I told her National & Provincial didn't have a branch there.

A lot of hard work had obviously gone into setting up the club and ground. The playing area had been cleared leaving it surrounded by trees, snug and picturesque. When I was there they had already drawn up plans for a clubhouse, and I'm sure that it will be of matching grandeur and style. Most of the members were expatriates on short or medium contracts, and not surprisingly I was invited to play for England & Wales against Ireland & Scotland, the local version of an international match, and contested with as much partisanship as if it was. I didn't get a cap, but I enjoyed it.

One of my fondest sporting memories was seeing Garfield Sobers hit Malcolm Nash for six sixes in an over at St Helen's in 1972. I remember it as if it were yesterday: taking the bus from Tumble to Swansea, clutching sandwiches and a flask of tea, as excited as only youth can be at the prospect of seeing Sobers, who was then and still is my greatest sporting hero. What a day to see him, the day when cricket history was written. I savoured it for years afterwards, and it was all the more poignant because, as Max Boyce would say, 'I was there'.

Imagine my surprise, my elation, when ages later I had the opportunity not only of meeting the great man, but of telling him that I'd seen his remarkable feat. That meeting, very special to me, came about because I had gone on a cricket tour, organised by 'Mr Travel Fixit', Fred Rumsey, to Barbados in 1983. I was there, not as much for my cricketing ability, which was questionable at the time, but as a rugby 'personality' in a team composed of celebrities: David Gower, Bill Athey, Trevor Bailey, Nick Cook, Ian Gould, Godfrey Evans, Tim Brooke-Taylor, Richard O'Sullivan, Robin Asquith, Ted Moult and Nicholas Parsons, to name but a few of a motley and variously talented lot of cricketers. Somehow, we won the tournament in which we played, and incredibly the man who presented the winning trophy was none other than Sir Garfield Sobers. We talked about his six sixes. Funny – he didn't mention my three sixes earlier in the day, out of the ground, over the bowler's head.

Apart from the cricket on that tour – and a similar one a year later – it was hardship all the way. There was the socialising, the parties, the golf, rum punch on the beach, water skiing, sunbathing, boat trips – Helen and I were really glad to get on the plane home! We left earlier than the main party. I had to play for Cardiff against Ebbw Vale the next day. You've got to get your priorities right, haven't you? I slept most of the flight back, but I was dog tired when we arrived at Heathrow at 9 am, and we still had the drive down the M4 ahead of us. We arrived in Cardiff at 1 pm, just in time to unpack, and for me, a quick cup of tea, and straight out on to the pitch in the rain on a cold November day. I was absolutely shattered at the end of the match. 'Never again' I promised, like a drunk on hangover morning. The next year I'd forgotten that promise. It was exactly the same – only this time the match against Ebbw Vale was up the valley, at Eugene Cross Park, muddy, wet and miserable. Oh, the things we players have to put up with!

'Money speaks sense in a language all nations understand'

Aphra Behn

14
THE FUTURE

There is a growing feeling that rugby football, if it is not professionalised already, is hurtling with powerful momentum in that direction. The World Cup, scheduled for 1987, may well become the watershed of the amateur game, with the controlling bodies unable to resist rewarding the participating players from the enormous sums that the tournament is likely to produce. Certainly they may 'dress up' the payments, they may describe them as out-of-pocket expenses or the like. But however vague their description, however unspecified their scope, once those payments are agreed and paid, amateur rugby as we know it will be finished.

The professed purists of the game will no doubt wage war against the advent of pro-rugby, but their voices, so strident in the past in keeping the sport pristinely amateur, are likely to be drowned out by the clink of money pouring into the Unions' cash drawers. The growth and increasing popularity of rugby throughout the world have made it a highly attractive vehicle for sponsorship and television, and inevitably the World Cup is going to be the biggest money-spinner the game has known. Rugby is no longer a game in the traditional sense, but a business, and the principles of business will guarantee the ultimate silence of the objectors. Money is only sordid when you haven't got it – when you've got a lot of it, as rugby certainly will have, it is quite a different matter. Suddenly the game will be in a position to do things it has never been able to do; not only will there be scope to build, say, superbly equipped multi-purpose stadiums, but there will be investment at all levels of the game, with gymnasiums, treatment and training facilities among the priorities which will change the face of the game. The payment of the leading players, the generators of the windfall, will seem insignificant by comparison.

It should not be underestimated how much rugby, particularly at grass roots, needs this cash, needs this development. In some countries, alternative forms of leisure have been enticing youngsters away from rugby in increasing numbers. The decline in the numbers taking up the game must be halted, and I suggest it would if rugby were to offer facilities to match those in other sports. The idea of the tin hut in a cowfield, with all its connotations, must be the target for eradication.

If the reasons for utilising the revenue from a World Cup are compelling, there are nevertheless some important questions which the governing bodies should consider. As a player nearing the end of his career, I have mixed feelings about payments for playing. Eddie Butler, the former captain of Wales, is right in arguing that the hypocrisy over such payments should end. In declaring unequivocally that the top players should be paid, even down to club level, he is voicing the opinion of many of them. Eddie, of course, is talking about things that have already happened, as much as what should happen in the future. It is worth pointing out that Eddie's views are a mirror of the opinions of the many top players who have discussed this, and other matters, for a very long time, essentially since David Lord put forward his private scheme for a World Cup. The decision by the International Board to stage their own World Cup merely accentuated the points of that dialogue. The difference was that Lord was offering players an incredible amount of money for playing. So far, the International Board have offered nothing.

This is the crux of the matter, to which the authorities must address themselves. They would be ill-advised to ignore it. If my personal concern is not the money that might or might not be available, this is not to say that all players would be prepared to forgo payment, and would simply play for the sake of honour or prestige, however unlikely that might be. What does concern me are the peripheral questions concerning the well-being of the players in *all* respects.

At the launch of *Rothmans Rugby Yearbook* in September 1985, after which I was widely quoted for my apparent views on the World Cup, my only motive in speaking out was to draw attention to some of the questions that it seemed no-one had asked. They were not views, or firm convictions, but questions. Let us consider the preparation of a side entering the World Cup. One has to assume that Wales, for instance, will want to mount a serious challenge and that they are not going to the Antipodes simply as a flag-waving exercise. This can only mean that their preparation is going to be serious. Regardless of what form that preparation may take, whether it would be week-long squad sessions, or fitness courses in Snowdonia, it will certainly be arduous and exacting. Quite clearly the demands on the players, once again, will multiply. I ask, is this right? Indeed, will they be *paid* to give of their time for preparation, which is extra-curricular in every sense?

Some will make the sacrifice and lose pay, or even their jobs. Is that just when the end product, the money generated by a World Cup, will run into millions. Is that amateurism?

As to the format of the tournament, no matter how they fiddle about with the preliminary matches, whether they play round robin groups or the like, it is conceivable that a side could play six matches in a period of three weeks. The argument that some of those matches will be less demanding and may not be of accepted international standard is superfluous. Regardless of the opposition, all the matches will place an enormous physical and mental strain on players, most of whom do not recover from an international match for at least a week. Again, has that been considered? Is the players' welfare being taken into account? Might there be extra matches, because of play-offs? What of injuries? What happens when a team, hit by injuries, have to play a match, say, which might be crucial in qualifying? Indeed, how many players will be taken in the first place? Will there be enough? Or, conversely, is it right that some players might travel as part of the squad and never play, which could happen?

Another area which, as a player, also concerns me, is the attitude that might be adopted because of the high motivation that a World Cup might impose. Let us say, for example, that two sides are contending for qualification, or a place in the semi-final. On one side there is an obvious star, a match-winner. Would he become a target for intimidation or a candidate for being taken out of the game altogether? How much pressure would be applied to players? Would the tournament become a nightmare, a travesty, with some teams adopting a win-at-all-costs attitude? Where, for instance, do referees fit into all this? What pressures will they have to endure in an important match, which they know is being televised all around the world?

I suppose the last consideration should concern the organisation of the World Cup. Any top marketing man will tell you that such a tournament has huge potential in producing revenue. Are our organisers equipped to realise this potential? Dare I ask it, are they *professional* enough to negotiate with international television moguls, sponsors and advertisers? Or will they call upon outside experts, who, for a fee or a percentage, will wring out every last penny from the event? If that is to be the case, is that not total undiluted professionalism and would the governing bodies be able to reconcile their motives *without* considering the players?

It would take a very clever man to provide all the answers to these questions, but they should be answered, should be discussed before the final go-ahead for the World Cup is given.

Provided these and other assurances are forthcoming, it seems to me that a World Cup presents an unequalled opportunity for rugby to step forward as a major world game. It could provide a marvellous show-piece, which would influence the developing countries and encourage the spread of the game. Commendable though that might be as a motive for staging the tournament, it is in itself insufficient reason if exploitation of the players is a consequence of it.

I realise that some people are cynical about the distance that rugby football has already travelled down the road towards professionalism. There are, of course, very good reasons why no-one yet has 'come clean' and admitted that he has not only broken the International Board regulations regarding professionalism but has driven a double decker bus right through them. The joke that Andy Haden has described his occupation as 'rugby player' on his passport in a sense obscures the fact that he has bent if not broken the rules and has admitted to so doing. Andy is still playing. He is still regarded as an amateur by the authorities in New Zealand, and no matter how the other member countries of the IB huff and puff, he will remain so for the very reason that the NZRFU have not cast him out into the wilderness.

There are players, of course, who have gone professional by turning to Rugby League; some of them have admitted, for example, that they were paid 'boot-money' and the like when they were amateurs, though I don't believe any of them found it necessary to 'rat' on players still playing Rugby Union to support their admissions. If the sceptics do not wish to believe these defectors (who, of course, no longer have anything to lose), what of the claim made, for instance, by David Lord that he entered into negotiations with many top players all over the world, which is in itself contrary to the amateur regulations? There are numerous other examples, other rumours and speculations, any of which, had they come to light 20 or even ten years ago, would have scandalised the game and would have evoked 'ban them' demands. Does this mean that today the game's guardians have given up trying to preserve rugby as a purely amateur sport? Are they turning the proverbial blind eye when they have circumstantial if not cast-iron evidence that the amateur rules are being flouted worldwide?

It is interesting that when Eddie Butler appealed for an end to hypocrisy over this matter and called for payments to players to be made openly, the WRU president Alun Thomas leapt to the defence of the amateur principles of the game. He totally rejected the idea that payments should be made to top players, reminding these players of their obligation and responsibility to the game. Whether that is the prevalent view within the WRU, or any other ruling body, is a moot point. It is possible that nothing has been done, or even seen to be done, because changes in the rules are imminent.

As someone nearing the end of his playing career, I am not envious that these changes will come too late in the day to affect me. To be candid, I've already had opportunities to make money out of the game. I rejected them, not because of blind adherence to amateur principles laid down long before today's administrators were born, but because the offers, although attractive, would have meant too great an upheaval in my private life.

I first became aware of what might be described as my 'commercial' value as a rugby player back in 1982 when Terry Holmes and I were invited to go to South Africa to play as a pair for Natal. The offer was initially for one season, and should all matters have proven satisfactory, it was to be extended to a permanent association. Let me say at once that this offer was of a very substantial nature, in cash and career terms, and Terry and I spent a long time discussing the relative merits of quitting Welsh rugby and playing in South Africa. Terry had turned down an incredible amount of money to turn to Rugby League, but his decision to say no to Natal was determined I believe by nothing less than patriotism: Cardiff, as always, held more appeal for Terry than the flesh-pots of South Africa. Natal promised us jobs – sinecures really – and accommodation, and while I found the offer attractive, I had to balance all this against what I would lose in terms of home, security and my job in Wales.

Coincidentally, an almost identical offer came my way from Western Province about the same time. They even assured me of a job with a building society in Cape Town. Naturally, I talked the matter over fully with my wife. I think what finally held me back was the concern that in effect one would be risking too much. There would be no contract and if, say, I suffered a serious injury as soon as I got there, I would end up with nothing. Helen and I were also very concerned about taking our daughter Kathryn to South Africa, particularly as their public order troubles seemed certain to increase.

If one ignores the David Lord bait, and a couple of other 'tempters', I suppose the next realistic offer came in 1984. The approach this time was from France, specifically the

Toulon club. It was made initially by Jerome Gallion, the French scrum-half, when he came to Cardiff to play in the Barbarians side which I captained against Australia. Jerome, Toulon's top player, was obviously instructed to sound me out. He made the idea sound very attractive indeed and as I love France, the food, the language, I was very tempted. A little later, the president of the Toulon club followed up Gallion's feeler and rang me at home to see whether I was interested. His English was not good, so the 'negotiations' were conducted by his daughter, who spoke English extremely well. Once again, the terms of the offer seemed marvellous at the time. The whole package would have given me in the region of £24,000 a year all found, and I was to have 'signed' for a minimum of two years. I have to concede that Toulon's offer was really an ego trip as far as I was concerned: it was pleasant to think that someone thought I was good enough to warrant that kind of financial commitment. It was, of course, a lot of money to pay someone just to play rugby. Suffice it to say, I once again said no. One of the deciding factors, I admit, was my concern over the lack of guarantees if I was injured, a worrying possibility, I thought, bearing in mind the very physical and hard nature of French club rugby.

Many of my contemporaries may find it puzzling that I have not cashed in on my rugby by taking up any of these offers. On balance, I think I have made the right decisions. As I have said elsewhere, rugby is no longer the most important thing in my life; my family, my home and my job have rightly superseded the pleasure I have derived from playing. If and when rugby does change in a commercial sense, I can visualise the day when players who say no will be the exception rather than the rule. I for one will neither blame them for wanting rewards nor envy them when they get them. I see no dishonour whatsoever in playing a sport at the very highest level and being paid for it. It's possible we might end up as a consequence with a game of higher quality and attractiveness.

Of one thing I'm certain, if the IB do not get their house in order as far as professionalism is concerned, events may overtake them. I'm thinking specifically of South Africa's situation with regard to the British Lions tour, which is scheduled to take place in the summer of 1986, but which is ever more doubtful because of the increase in the unrest in the Republic and the growing condemnation worldwide of the country's political leadership. In the present circumstances, there is no choice. The Lions will *not* go, and that will mean but one thing: professionalism in one form or another will start in South Africa in 1986. One assumes that the IB must realise that plans to replace the Lions tour with a professional tournament are already drawn up. Even if the South African Rugby Board are claiming no participation in such a tournament, that must be interpreted as diplomatic evasion, nothing more. The South African rugby authorities have admitted knowledge of the formation of several companies who intend to run the professional tournament and, even if they wanted to, they would be powerless to prevent such a tournament taking place.

Several prominent South African businessmen are purported to be behind the scheme, and one such person frequently mentioned is Robert Denton, the managing director of Ellis Park Stadium in Johannesburg. According to the 'propagandists' who have been infiltrating the UK and other countries ever since New Zealand pulled out of their 1985 tour, the highly influential Denton is involved in the setting up of professional companies in Pretoria and Cape Town. The UK reaction seems to be dismissive – 'we will not be blackmailed' – but I have learned from several players, who intend to be closely involved, that once the formal thumbs down for the Lions tour is made public, the professional tournament will be announced. And it will take place.

Let us make no mistake about the feasibility of a professional tournament in South Africa. Money will be no stumbling block, as it has been with the projects of David Lord and others. The vested interests in South Africa are in a position to underwrite all expenses and can offer immense sums to players. I daresay only a few of the world's top players will have the reason or the will not to succumb to such temptation.

A professional tournament in South Africa, regardless of its format, has all the ingredients of a viable venture. The stadiums are there, so is a captive audience, and the interested parties have already established contacts with several top-class players in various countries throughout the world. I found it of passing interest to listen in to a couple of these players discussing the relative merits of the tournament at, of all places, Twickenham, in October 1985, after I had played there for Cardiff against Harlequins. Suffice it to say, players needed little convincing that a tournament will take place, echoing perhaps the views of Morne du Plessis, the Springbok captain, who has declared it 'inevitable' that the game will go professional. The only question is, which players will make up the touring party, who will be the performers in the circus?

Personally, I doubt if I would go if invited, regardless of the money that would be offered. As I have matured in the game, as I have got older, my attitude has changed. While I will always defend the right of any sportsman to make his own choice about whether he should or should not go to South Africa, I feel that I am no longer susceptible to being tempted to play there again. I have been profoundly affected by the daily mayhem in South Africa, and appalled by the news of the deaths of so many people. It may be a combination of that abhorrence and my maturity which has steered me away from the possibility of ever playing there again. The money simply does not come into it. It doesn't seem right that one should be kicking some leather to delight a crowd-packed stadium while a couple of miles away people are being shot because they are protesting against injustice.

Other players, however, might have no such pangs of conscience, particularly if the organisers are bent on covering up payments so as to 'protect' the players' amateur status. It seems to me that the major problem the organisers face is not enticing the world's top players, but giving them an identity as a team, providing them with a sense of belonging, of pride in their performance. Whenever I have played for invitation sides in South Africa, these elements have been lacking and, for the tournament to be meaningful, it would be essential that they were a part of the tourists' make-up. It is conceivable that this could be achieved by offering, say, appearance money and then doubling it or trebling it as an incentive for winning and playing well. Exhibition matches will not work, but matches in which the Springboks' reputation is at stake, when either victory or defeat is not a foregone conclusion, are sure to fill the stadiums and give the tour credibility.

It is possible, too, that if such a tournament proved to be successful, the format could be adopted elsewhere. How many people would bet against a highly motivated – and well paid – XV comprising the world's best players filling stadiums in the UK, for instance, or in Australia or New Zealand? It is pertinent to recall that when the lawn tennis professional circus started, no-one thought it would get off the ground let alone endure. Look at it now. The game is a highly profitable and successful operation throughout the world – and there was a time, not so long ago, when lawn tennis adhered to pure amateurism with as much passion as rugby, if not more.

Such eventualities, of course, would pose an immediate and an ongoing threat to the structure of the game, particularly in the IB countries, and inevitably would have a devaluing effect on the IB's projected World Cup in 1987. Indeed, one might well ask whether the IB would go ahead with the World Cup if, say, the cream of the world's players cast their lot with a South African-orientated professional circus. Many countries who have accepted the invitation to play in the World Cup have only done so, it seems, under some duress and have insisted upon certain assurances. Their resolve and enthusiasm for the controversial World Cup, which is already clearly tenuous, might vanish if they discovered they had to compete in Australia and New Zealand without their best players. Moreover, would the television companies and sponsors feel as enthusiastic about the project if the 'stars' were missing? Would the World Cup be viable if the carpet of financial guarantees was suddenly pulled from underneath the organisers? Indeed, one can but wonder about the unanimity of attitude of the member countries of the IB if they were confronted by a realistic alternative professional tournament. Can any of rugby's governing bodies be absolutely sure that *all* the countries would close ranks and defend amateur principles? Is it not an intriguing possibility that some countries might actually welcome the alternative and throw their lot in, say, with a South Africa determined that rugby football, paid or otherwise, will survive?

I feel barely qualified to offer answers to these questions, or solutions to the problems that might arise out of the birth of professional rugby in South Africa. It seems to me that they are the province, and should be the priority, of the governors of our game. However, conjecture does not cloud my views about matters closer to home, as it were. As this book was being completed, the state of the game in Wales was under closer scrutiny than it had been for some time, with many observers lamenting the apparent decline in standards at every level, and particularly in first-class rugby. As someone still closely involved in the club scene, I had a vested interest in this expression of concern for the game in Wales. It seemed to me a spontaneous reaction, particularly among the media, rather than any conspiratorial desire to 'have a go' at the authorities. Everyone declared a genuine worry about the game's decline, with the way clubs were playing being presented as a yardstick of the malaise.

As someone who does not often agree with the game's critics, let me say at once that they did a very good job in bringing the matter into the public arena. The murmurings and rumblings had been going on in every Welsh clubhouse for some time, and the media reacted responsibly in mirroring views and concern as the 1985-86 season entered its third month. As a player, I unhesitatingly agreed with the observation that matches had lacked sparkle, and players had looked jaded and tired. To make a personal point: of the first 15 matches I played for Cardiff, I can honestly say I enjoyed only one of them, and that was because it was a rather light-hearted affair, against Harlequins, in a free and easy atmosphere at Twickenham. If my personal lack of enjoyment and fulfilment was multiplied across the whole spectrum of the first-class club game in Wales, as it might be, then we have one of the explanations for the gloom-and-doom comments that abounded as the season got underway. If matches were dull and dour for those that watched, I can only say that it was much the same for the players. I can't think of any player who had had any sustained fun since the season kicked off in September. If someone had come up to me to tell me that he had enjoyed playing, I would have assumed he was on drugs or something. It was dreadful. Unadulterated boredom on the field, and post-mortems of despair off it.

Everyone, of course, was ready with an explanation for the demise of the Welsh game as witnessed in the first couple of months of the 1985-86 season. Predictably, coaching and coaches took the brunt of the blame. Static rucking and mauling was also criticised, the lack of flair and basic skill was bemoaned. Quality subdued by quantity was another common observation. The most telling comment, however, in my view, concerned the number of matches in which players were required to take part. There is no doubt in my mind that they are playing far too often, and that their staleness and lack of enthusiasm is entirely due to the Wednesday-Saturday syndrome which no other player in world rugby is asked to endure. This twice-a-week madness is underlined when compared with the playing requirements of a country such as New Zealand. There a player might feel overplayed if he participates in 20 matches in a season, while in Wales some people will have played that many in the first two months. It is ludicrous – absolute folly. And it is indefensible. To my mind, the over-playing of players *is* the root cause of the decline in standards, and I'm sure the situation will deteriorate further until something is done to end these excessive demands. The game is sliding downhill fast, and unless the clubs themselves urgently address themselves to this problem in particular, they might find themselves not only without spectators wanting to watch, but without players wanting to play. Instead of having the so-called difficulty of cutting fixtures, they might find themselves with no fixtures at all.

I wish Cardiff, for instance, would take the lead in this matter. As the premier Welsh club I'm sure they'd be respected if, at a stroke, they decided enough was enough, and immediately slashed their fixture list by half, cutting out the mid-week matches and playing only on Saturdays. Obviously such a move would be regarded with horror and dismay by some, particularly by clubs who would find themselves deprived of what they regard as their plum fixture. My answer to the wails of treasurers moaning about the curtailment of income is that once Saturday resumes as the major club rugby day, any mid-week loss of revenue would be made up once the Saturday fixtures again became the number one attraction for spectators. A case in point was the eccentricity of Cardiff's fixtures in October 1985. In a two-week period, we played Pontypool, Wasps, Bath and Harlequins, with the prime fixtures, Bath and Pontypool, absurdly, taking place in the mid-week. With deference to Wasps and Quins, the major matches against Bath and Pontypool should have been played on Saturday. I realise that traditional fixtures are coveted in most senior clubs, but in maintaining them and thereby increasing the number of matches played in mid-week, the clubs have stretched their playing resources beyond common sense. Players quite honestly cannot cope. They cannot be motivated to play more than once a week, nor should they be required to do so. Going up to Bath the players to a man groaned at the prospect. 'What are we doing here?' they all asked resignedly. Terry Holmes, the most loyal player Cardiff has ever had, went even further. He declared that that was the last time that he would play away long distance in mid-week. I understood exactly how he felt. When someone like Holmesy declares himself 'out', then Cardiff ought to sit up and take notice.

There is, of course, an alternative to chopping mid-week matches. As they did once before, I believe in the 'fifties, Cardiff could effectively field two sides, not for Saturdays only as they did then, but one for the mid-week and one for Saturday. It might present a few problems over fixtures, but certainly the playing members would appreciate such a move.

In the end, however, I suppose the solution rests with the players themselves. I'm not advocating Player Power, but if the senior players in each club got together and issued an ultimatum stating that they were prepared to play only once a week, then presumably the club would be under some pressure to observe their wishes. Imagine the furore if, for instance, Holmesy, myself, Bob Norster, Alan Phillips, John Scott, Jeff Whitefoot, Ian Eidman, Gareth Roberts and Adrian Hadley decided to veto mid-week matches as a matter of principle. The club, obviously, would either accept our stand, or ask us all politely to make our beds elsewhere. If all other senior players followed suit, and they were also requested by their clubs to seek other pastures, what a fascinating situation we'd have. One thing is certain – the fixture lists would *have* to be halved, unless, of course, the committee men took it upon themselves to become Golden Oldies.

CAREER STATISTICS

GARETH DAVIES'S CAREER RECORD WITH CARDIFF 1974-1985

Season	*Matches*	*T*	*C*	*DG*	*PG*	*Pts*
1974-75	21	2	25	3	24	139
1975-76	32	5	40	3	41	232
1976-77	22	4	41	3	17	158
1977-78	14	1	19	1	18	99
1978-79	30	10	62	7	30	275
1979-80	27	5	51	7	28	227
1980-81	29	6	39	7	47	264
1981-82	35	6	35	3	29	190
1982-83	29	10	47	3	13	182
1983-84	35	9	82	8	53	383†
1984-85	31	5	81	8	53	365
Total	305	63	522	53	353	2514

Tour matches						
South Africa 1979	6	—	11	1	12	61
Zimbabwe 1981	5	2	8	—	13	63
Italy 1975-76	2	2	2	—	2	18
South Africa 1982	5	1	1	—	11	39
Thailand 1984	3	3	23	—	—	58
Total	21	8	45	1	38	239

†club record total

Record against British clubs

	Matches	*T*	*C*	*DG*	*PG*	*Pts*
Barbarians	10	2	29	—	8	90
Bath	3	1	2	—	2	14
Bective Rangers	1	—	—	—	—	—
Bedford	2	1	6	—	1	19
Bristol	14	3	20	2	20	118
Camborne	1	—	1	—	—	2
Cambridge U	2	—	6	1	2	21
Coventry	12	7	30	—	11	121
Gala	1	—	—	—	2	6
Gloucester	4	3	2	—	6	34
Harlequins	7	—	14	—	7	49
Headingley	1	—	2	1	2	13
Leicester	1	2	4	—	—	16
Moseley	10	2	24	—	12	92
Munster	2	—	2	1	3	16
Garryowen	1	—	1	—	1	5
New Brighton	1	—	1	—	1	5
Northampton	7	1	16	1	6	57
Orrell	1	—	3	—	4	18
Oxford U	4	1	9	—	5	37
St Ives	1	—	—	—	—	—
Saracens	1	—	—	—	2	6
Penzance	1	—	—	—	—	—
Wasps	1	—	3	—	—	6
Total	89	23	175	6	95	745

Record against Welsh clubs

	Matches	*T*	*C*	*DG*	*PG*	*Pts*
Aberavon	18	2	23	2	23	129
Abertillery	1	1	1	—	1	9
Bridgend	15	1	11	2	24	104
Cross Keys	1	1	2	—	2	14
Ebbw Vale	14	7	33	4	9	133
Glam Wands	5	—	9	—	9	45
Llanelli	17	2	13	2	24	112
London Welsh	9	2	15	2	8	68
Maesteg	5	—	5	—	10	40
Neath	16	2	19	3	17	106
Newbridge	6	1	6	2	7	43
Newport	14	2	20	3	22	123
Penarth	6	2	28	1	3	76
Pontypool	18	3	9	9	27	138
Pontypridd	15	3	22	4	22	134
Swansea	18	2	20	8	25	147
Tredegar	1	—	1	—	—	2
Total	179	31	237	42	233	1423

Other matches

	Matches	T	C	DG	PG	Pts
Second class sides in Cup*	17	3	54	—	12	156
Australia	2	1	1	1	3	18
New Zealand	2	—	—	3	1	12
Maoris	1	—	—	—	—	—
Argentina	1	—	2	—	3	13
Canada	1	—	2	—	1	7
Italy XV	1	—	7	—	—	14
Overseas XV	1	—	2	—	—	4
Crawshay's Welsh	2	2	6	—	3	29
Glasgow & District	1	—	2	1	1	10
Irish Wolfhounds	1	—	1	—	1	5
East District	3	2	24	—	—	56
Llandaff	1	—	1	—	—	2
Nice	1	1	4	—	—	12
L'Aquila (Italy)	1	—	2	—	—	4
Slaminio (Italy)	1	—	2	—	—	4
Total	37	9	110	5	25	346

**Gorseinon, Aberaman, Cardiff College of Education, Whitland, Crumlin, Waunarlwydd, Wrexham, Tonyrefail (2), British Steel Port Talbot, Barry, Cilfynydd, Gowerton, Blackwood, Senghenydd, Treorchy, Bryncoch.*

GARETH DAVIES'S INTERNATIONAL CAREER

Date	*Match*	*Venue*	*Result*	*T*	*C*	*DG*	*PG*	*Pts*
11 Jun 1978	Australia	Brisbane	L 8-18	—	—	—	—	—
17 Jun 1978	Australia	Sydney	L 17-19	—	—	1	2	9
11 Nov 1978	N. Zealand	Cardiff	L 12-13	—	—	—	3	9
20 Jan 1979	Scotland	Murrayfield	W 19-13	—	—	—	—	—
3 Feb 1979	Ireland	Cardiff	W 24-21	—	—	—	—	—
17 Feb 1979	France	Paris	L 13-14	—	—	—	—	—
17 Mar 1979	England	Cardiff	W 27-3	—	—	1	—	3
6 Oct 1979	Romania	Cardiff	W 13-12	—	—	2	—	6
19 Jan 1980	France	Cardiff	W 18-9	—	1	—	—	2
16 Feb 1980	England	Twickenham	L 8-9	—	—	—	—	—
1 Mar 1980	Scotland	Cardiff	W 17-6	—	—	—	—	—
1 Nov 1980	N. Zealand	Cardiff	L 3-23	—	—	—	—	—
17 Jan 1981	England	Cardiff	W 21-19	—	—	1	—	3
7 Feb 1981	Scotland	Murrayfield	L 6-15	—	—	—	—	—
5 Dec 1981	Australia	Cardiff	W 18-13	—	—	1	—	3
23 Jan 1982	Ireland	Dublin	L 12-20	—	—	—	—	—
6 Feb 1982	France	Cardiff	W 22-12	—	—	—	—	—
6 Mar 1982	England	Twickenham	L 7-17	—	—	1	—	3
20 Mar 1982	Scotland	Cardiff	L 18-34	—	—	—	—	—
2 Mar 1985	Scotland	Murrayfield	W 25-21	—	—	1	—	3
16 Mar 1985	Ireland	Cardiff	L 9-21	—	1	1	—	5
30 Mar 1985	France	Paris	L 3-14	—	—	—	—	—
Total				0	2	9	5	46

British Lions appearances

				T	*C*	*DG*	*PG*	*Pts*
14 Jun 1980	South Africa	Bloemfontein	L 19-26	—	1	—	2	8
Total				0	3	9	7	54

INDEX

Figures in Roman numerals indicate pagination of illustrated section between text pages

Aberaeron Sevens 83
Aberavon 37, 57, 86, 87, 97
Abertillery 57
Abertillery Park 96
Aberystwyth 37, 52, 125, 128
Abraham, William 35
Ackerman, Bob 19, vi, viii
Amsterdam 150
Angel Hotel, Cardiff 88
A.N. Other 15-17
Arfryn 39
Ashworth, John 148
Asquith, Robin 152
Athey, Bill 152
Atlantic All Stars 138
Auckland 131
Australia 24, 27, 29, 38, 51, 54, 66, 79, 92-5, 126, 129, 130, 138-40, 144, 145, 160, 163

Bailey, Trevor 152
Ballymena 72
Ballymore 144
Baird, Roger viii
Bangkok 150
Baptist Chapel, Tumble 40, 41
Barbados 150-2, xii
Barbarians 10, 21, 29, 70, 71, 75, 82, 96, 111, 134-140, 142-4, 160, xvi
Bath 30, 166
BBC 84, 140
Beard, Roger 63
Beattie, Jock 101
Beaumont, Bill 140
Bennett, Phil 25, 28, 57, 58, 93, 94, 113, 117, 119
Bethesda Road, Tumble 32
Bevan, John 15, 18-20, 125, 132
Billot, John 108
Bishop Hannon School 81, 85
Blaenurwen colliery 42
Blaina 88
Blanco, Serge 121, 139
Bloemfontein 146, 147, x
Boniface, André 106
Bosch, Gerald vii
Boston Bicentennial Tournament 138
Boston College 144
Botha, Naas 121, 147, ix
Bowes, Stan 64, 65
Boyce, Max 50, 151
Brace, Onllwyn 74
Brain's Beers 61, 62, 78, 84, 135
Brewery Field 49
Bridgend 49
Brisbane 38, 39, 92
Bristol 72, 92
British Lions 10, 26, 64, 82, 101, 102, 119, 128, 142, 145-7, 161, x (2), xi, xiv (2)
Brooke-Taylor, Tim 152
Bryan, Tim 77, 78
Buckley's Brewery 41
Budd, Zola 88
Bukta 85
Bulawayo 89
Burcher, David iii
Burgess, Clive 17
Burnley Building Society 11
Bush, Percy 110
Burton, Mickey 92, 93
Butcher's Arms pub 104, 105
Butler, Eddie 23, 78, 155, 158
Butterfield, Jeff 105

Café Royal 78
Calder, Jim viii
Camberabero, Lilian & Guy 48
Cambridge University 71, 75, 78, 111
Cameron, Angus 106
Campbell, Ollie 146
Canada 70-2, 74, 138, 140, 142, 144
Cannell, Lewis 106
Cannon, Steve 109
Canterbury 131
Canton, Cardiff 70
Cape Town 159, 161
Cardiff 34, 37, 49, 57, 69, 70, 78, 82, 96, 97, 135, 139, 152, 159, 160
Cardiff Arms Park 10, 17, 22, 24-6, 48, 49, 58, 66, 70, 85, 88, 91, 95, 96, 104, 106, 109, 111, 137, 138, ii, iii, viii
Cardiff Centenary 74, 138
Cardiff Civic Centre 70
Cardiff RFC 10, 15, 18, 19, 24, 27-30, 36, 55-67, 70, 72, 74, 76, 79, 82, 84-9, 91-100, 102, 104, 106-11, 116-18, 127, 128, 131, 132, 138, 143, 145, 148-50, 152, 165-7, ii (2), iii, ix
Cardiff Sports Centre 127
Cardiff Youth 81, 84, 87
Carmarthen 32, 57
Carmarthen Athletic 57
Carmarthenshire RU 10, 57
Caroline Street, Cardiff 69
Carson, Willie 140
Cathay's, Cardiff 70, 71
Caussade, Alain 25
Cayman Islands 150
Cefneithin 71
Celaya, Michel 104
Centre Hotel, Cardiff 29
Charlton, Jackie & Bobby 49
Cholley, Gerard 25
Clarke, Don vii
Clifton-Taylor, Alec 33
coaching conference 127-30
Cobner, Terry 19
Coleman, David 140
Colston, Peter 92
Comrades Marathon 146
Connors, Mick 73
Cook, Nick 152
Cooper, Dr P.F. 105
Cordle, Gerald 86
Cotton, Fran 26, 92, 93, 147, x
Coventry RFC 52
Cowley St John School 78
Crawshay's Welsh 148, 149
Crest International Hotel, Brisbane 39
Cross Hands 49
Cross Hands Working Men's Club 53
Cromwell, Richard & Oliver 39
Cuba 150
Cwmcelyn 88
Cynheidre Colliery 34, 42

Dacey, Malcolm 15, 16, 19, 109, xiii
Damascus 150
Daniels, Pat iii
Davies, Dai 37
Davies, D.E. 55
Davies, Elvet 11, 32, 33, 38, 42, 43, 45-9, v
Davies, Evan 38
Davies, Mrs Elvet 11, 41, 46, 47, 49, v
Davies, Gary 65

Davies, Gerald 29, 59, 62, 63, 86, 94-6, 122, 127
Davies, Glyn iii
Davies, Helen 11, 14, 16, 32, 53, 57, 74, 78, 79, 81, 83, 150-2, 159, iv, xii
Davies, Huw 64
Davies, John 59, 85, 106
Davies, Jonathan 16, 50, 51, 117
Davies, Kathryn 32, 42, 66, 83, 159, iv, v (2)
Davies, Lynn 38
Davies, Mel 59
Davies, Mervyn 127
Davies, S.O. 35
Davies, Twm Casken Bach 41
Davies, Windsor xiii
Davies, W.P.C. 105
Dawes, John 14, 18, 20, 24, 126, 127, 130
Dawson, Les 140
Deans, Colin viii
De Maid, Matthew iii
Dench, Judi 72
Denton, Robert 161
Devil's Bridge 144
Domec, Henri 104
Donovan, Alun 17, 87
Drefach 36
Dufau, Georges 106
du Plessis, Morne 162
Dupuy, Jean 106
Durban 64, 146
Durham, Bishop of 41

Eastern Province 145, xi
East India & Sports Club 135
Ebbw Vale 116, 152
Ebenezer Chapel, Tumble 32, 41
Edwards, Gareth 25, 29, 46, 48, 58-62, 82, 93, 94, 110, 117, 127, 138, 149
Edwards, Kevin 88, 89
Eidman, Ian 87, 88, 167, iii
El Grec's, Cardiff 69, 78
Ella, Mark 129
Elliott, Paul iii
Ellis Park Stadium 161
England, 15, 24-6, 37, 48, 50, 51, 76, 91-6, 101, 102, 104, 105, 127, 132, vi, xv
England-Wales XV 26
Eugene Cross Park 96, 152
Evans, Emrys 37
Evans, Godfrey 152
Evans, Gwyn vii
Evans, Ieuan 124
Evans, John 88
Evans, Paul 92
Evans, Thiophilous 36
Ewing, Bobby 145

Farmoor 76, 77
Farnham Park 77
Felinfoel 41
Fenwick, Steve 17, 26, 27, 144, vi
Ferguson, Gordon 139
Fiji 131, 132
Finlayson, Alex 62
Floodlight Alliance 130
France 25, 48, 104-6, 121, 129, 159, vii
Francis, Albert 10, 84
Frankfurt 150

Gallion, Jerome 139, 160
Georgetown (Cayman Islands) 151
Germany 76
Gibson, Mike 25
Glamorgan CCC 53
Gloucester 66
Gloucestershire 92
Gnoll, The 98
Golding, Owen 98, iii
Goldsworthy, Mike 110
Gould, Ian 152
Gower, David 152, xii
Grand Cayman 150
Grand Slam 25, 48, 101, 104, 125
Gravell, Ray 17, 144, 147
Great Britain Rugby League XV 38
Great Mountain Pit 34, 35, 37, 40, 42
Great Mountain Working Men's Club 41
Greer, Germaine 83
Gregson, Dai 69
Gren 33
Greville, Handel 38, 51, 59
Griffiths, James 35
Guardian, The 72, 73
Gwelo 149
Gwendraeth Brewery 41
Gwendraeth Grammar School 10, 44-54, 69, 71

Haden, Andy 158
Hadley, Adrian 86, 167
Hancock, Frank 66
Hands, David 16
Hardiman, Bill 10
Hare, Dusty 25, 26, 53
Harlequins 162, 164, 166
Harris-Jones, Frank 71, 72
Harse, Keith 63
Harvard University 144
Hawick 139
Hayward, Dai 64
Heathrow 147, 152
Heol y Bryn, Tumble 32-4
Herdman, Jeff 135, 136
Hignell, Alistair 93
Holley, Tom 97, iii
Holmes, Sue 81, 83
Holmes, Terry 14, 16, 24-6, 29, 49, 60, 62-4, 81-5, 87-9, 94, 99, 100, 117, 118, 121, 122, 143, 146, 147, 149, 159, 166, 167, ii (2), iii, iv, x
Hopkins, Ken 73-6, 78
Horse & Groom pub 139
Hughes, Mark 50
Hutchings, Neil ii

Iffley Road 77
Inniskillen Dragoons 42
International Board 155, 158, 160, 163
Inyanga Mountains 149
Ireland 24, 26, 27, 37, 48, 104-6, viii
Italy 111

Jackson, Peter 106
James, Carwyn 45, 49-51, 72, 74
James, Keith 57, 58
Jan Smuts Airport 145
Jeeps, Dickie 106
Jeffrey, Howard 69
Jenkins, Gareth 144
Jenkins, Vivian 36
Johannesburg 145, 146, 161, xiv
John, Barry 46, 48, 50, 51, 57, 61, 71, 108-10, 113, 127, xiii
John, Nancy & Ted 65, 66
Jones, Des 37, 51
Jones, Glan 74
Jones, Gwynoro 35
Jones, Ken (Llanelli) 50
Jones, Ken (Newport) 105
Jones, Les 53
Jones, P.L. 62
Jones, Roger 71, 72
Jones, Wil Ardwyn 37
Jones, Winston 131

Karachi 150
Keane, Moss 139
Kennedy, John 108
Kiernan, Mike viii
Knight, Laurie 119
Knill, Mike 82
Kyle, Jackie 106

Lakin, Bobby 87
Lampeter 85
Lane, Roger 62
Lane, Stuart 116, 145, 146
Lawn Tennis 163
Laws, the 131-3
Lease, Brian 87
Leicester 138
Lewis, Allan 57

Lewis, Malcolm 14
Lewis, Rhodri 17, iii, vi
Light, Byron 74-6, 78
Liverpool 132
Llandaff 104
Llandaff Cathedral 32
Llandovery College 52
Llanelli 10, 28, 29, 32, 36-8, 40, 42, 50, 52, 57-9, 61, 70, 77, 107, 108, 132, 144
Llanelli & Mynydd Mawr Railway 35, 41, 42
Llannon Parish Council 39
Llannon village 42
Lloyd, Chris 50
Lloyd, John 18, 20
Lloyd George, Lady Megan 35
Lloyd's Bank, Tumble 33
Loftus Versfeldt 148, ix
London Scottish 78
London Welsh 76, 77, 137
Lord, David 155, 158, 159, 161
Lord's Taverners xii
Luff, John 92

Manchester 85
Manchester United 50
Matthews, David 132
Matthews, Gary 86
McBride, Willie John 102
McGeechan, Ian 25, 138, 143
McKechnie, Brian 24
McLauchlan, Ian 25
Mersey Tunnel 41
Merthyr 71
Miami 150
Middleton, Rob 69
Midland Bank, Tumble 33
Millar, Syd 101, 148
Mogridge, Tony iii
Moir, Malcolm 78
Monmouthshire 57
Montreal 144
Monty's, Cardiff 69
Mordell, Bob 93, 94
Mordt, Ray 121
Morgan, Cliff 105
Morgan, Derek 96
Morgan, Joe 108
Morgan, Luther 50
Morgan, Peter 147
Morgan, Robert 51
Morgan, Rod 16
Moseley 57, 66, 67
Moult, Ted 152
Murphy, Mike 62, 116, 117
Murrayfield 24, 27, 49, 106, vi
Mynydd Mawr Schools 10, 52

Nash, Malcolm 151, xii
Natal 64, 145, 148, 159
Natal Country XV 64
National & Provincial Building Society 11, 33, 151
Navratilova, Martina 50
Neath 37, 65, 98
Nefyn Williams, T. 35, 41
Nelmes, Barry 62, 91-6, iii
Newbridge 18, 96
Newcastle (Natal) 54
Newlands 148, xv
Newman, Bob ii
Newport 29, 65, 72, 74, 88, 92, 138
New Zealand 24, 26, 85, 88, 94, 102, 119, 121, 128, 129, 131, 148, 158, 161, 163, 165, ii, iii, vii, xv
Niagara Falls 144
Noble, Dr Clive 146, 147
Norling, Clive 132
Norris, Howard 59, 64
Norster, Robert 88, 167, iii
Northampton RFC 52
North Free State 87
North Wales 57
Nyhan, Peter 64, 65

Old Deer Park 76
Oldham RL 38
Orrell 57
O'Reilly, Tony 106
O'Sullivan, Richard 152
Owen, Garfield 104, 105
Oxford University 10, 37, 54, 74-9, 95

Pakistan Airlines 150
Paradise Curry House 62
Paris xii
Parsons, Nicholas 152
Pattaya Beach 150
Pat Pong 150
Patterson, Colin 146, xiv
Pedlow, Cecil 106
Pembrokeshire 84
Penarth 28, 58
Penylan, Cardiff 70
Phillips, Alan 17, 18, 61, 62, 65, 85, 87, 92, 94, 149, 167
Phillips, William 40
Pietersmaritsburg 146
Pokere, Steve 121, 148
Pontyberem iv
Pontyberem HS 52
Pontypool RFC 30, 81, 82, 101, 107, 109, 110, 166
Pontypool Front Row 93
Pontypool Park 76, 82, 109
Pontypridd 59, 128
Port Elizabeth 145, 146, xi, xiv
Prat, Jean 104
Preece, Derek iii
Pretoria 148, 161
Pretoria Defence 116
Pretoria Police ix
Pretoria Royal Infirmary 117
Price, Graham 23, 25, 144
professionalism 157-67
Putney Bridge 42
Pyle RFC 86, 92

Quebec 138, 144
Question of Sport 140
Quinnell, Derek 23, 25, 101, iv
Qui Qui's, Cardiff 69

Reddings, The 67
Rees, Elgan 25
Rees, Enoch 35
Rees, John 150
Rees, Mrs 71
Rees, Paul (Pablo) 83, 86, 116, 143
Rees, Paul (journalist) 108
Rees, Peter 38, 51
referees 131-3
Renwick, Jim xv
RFU Handbook 135
Rhondda, The 69
Rhosnewydd estate 32
Richards, Dai 23, 25-7, 114, 138, 146, 147, vi, x
Richards, Dr Melville 39
Richardson, John 97
Ring, Mark 86, 87, 109
Ringer, Paul 25, 101
Rives, Jean-Pierre 25
Robbie, John 78
Roberts, Evan 40
Roberts, Gareth 87, 167
Robinson, Ian 62, 138, 143
Rodney Parade 18, 30, 72
Romania 25, 111
Rosslyn Park 93, 96
Rothmans Rugby Yearbook 156
Rowe Williams, L. 35, 41
Rowlands, Keith 59
Royal Bangkok Sporting Club 150
Royal Hotel, Cardiff 135, 138
Rugby League 38, 158, 159
Rugby Special 86
Rumsey, Colleen and Fred 150, 151, xii
Rutherford, John 117, 121, vi
Ryan, John 63, 64, 129

Salisbury (Zimbabwe) 149
Sanson, Norman 94
Saskatchewan 138
Sasolberg 87

Scargill, Arthur 43
Scotland 17, 24-27, 37, 49, 104, 106, 121, vi, viii
Scotland-Ireland XV 26
Scott, John 87, 91, 93, 94, 96-102, 129, 142, 143, 167, iii, vi, xv
Shaw, Mark 148, xv
Skym, Archie 36, 37
Slemen, Mike 146
Smith, Ann & Barry 151
Smith, Arthur 106
Smyth, Dave 72
Snowdonia 156
Sobers, Sir Garfield 151, 152, xii
South Africa 26, 64, 76, 87, 89, 99, 101, 116, 121, 142, 145-9, 159, 160-4, vii, ix, x (2), xi, xiv
South African Rugby Board 161
South African Universities 111
South Glamorgan Constabulary 37
South Wales Echo 33, 83
South Wales Police 15
Squire, Jeff 23, 25, 101, 102, iv
Squires, Peter 25
Stade Colombes 104
Stanley, Bob 11
Stephens, Ian vi
St Catherine's College 77
St David's RFC (Cardiff & Pembrokeshire) 84
St Edmund Hall 78
St Helen's 151, xii
St Luke's College 96, 101
St Pierre xiii (2)
Stone, Alan 53
Stradey Park 57-9, 77
Stratford 72
Swansea 30, 59, 65, 66, 86, 87, 109, 114, 132, 135, 138, 151, iii
Swansea University 73, 74
Swift, Tony 87
Sydney (Australia) 92, 144

Talbot Athletic Ground 97
Thailand 65, 150
Thomas, Alun 158
Thomas, Brian 37
Thomas, Eifion 53
Thomas, 'Gym' 52
Thomas, Kevin 148
Thomas, Malcolm 105
Thomas, Watcyn 36
Tiger Bay 65, 70
Times, The 17
Tonga 57
Toulon 160
Traherne Hall 70-2
Transvaal 146
Triple Crown 24, 25, 125, iv
Troutbeck 149
Tumble Hotel, the 33, 38
Tumble Inn, the 39, 40
Tumble Primary School 10, 47, i
Tumble RFC 10, 29, 33, 36-39, 50, 54, 84
Tumble Strike, the 42
Tumble village 11, 32-43, 57, 69, 71, 108, 151, i
Twickenham 25, 36, 49, 73, 74, 77, 91-5, 101, 111, 137, 162, 164

UAU 73
Ulster 72
Underwood, Rory 139
University Match, the 49, 76-9, 111
USA 138, 144
Usk 65
UWIST 10, 57, 69-75, 78, 143

Vanderbijl Park xiv
Van Heerden, Moaner 116, 117
Vannier, Maurice 106
Victoria Falls 149
Villepreux, Pierre xii
Vincent's Club 78

Waddell, Herbert 135
Waddell, John 41
Wales, 10, 14-20, 22-9, 36-8, 45, 48-50, 54, 70, 76, 79, 82, 84, 86-9, 91, 93-5, 101, 104, 105, 125, 140, 143-5, 155, 156, 164, 165, ii, iv, vi (2), vii, viii (2)
Wales Football Team 50
Wallace, Gerry 62
Walters, Daniel 35
Ward, Tony 146
Wasps 73, 166
Watkins, David 88
Watkins, Mike (Spikey) 23, 85, 139, 143, iii
Watkinson, Tony 78
Webber, Chris ii
Welsh County Championship 57
Welsh Cup 18, 28, 30, 58, 61, 74, 87, 100, 128, 129
Welsh Rugby Union 14, 16, 26, 84, 125, 128, 158, xiii
Welsh Secondary Schools Rugby 10, 24, 49, 51, 57
Welsh Secondary Schools Cricket 53
Welsh Youth 49
Western Province 148, 159, xv
Western Valley 88
West Germany 111
West Wales RU 37
Whetton, Gary 121
Whitefoot, Jeff 87, 88, 167, iii
Williams, Brynmor 26, 29, 59, 60, 62, 82, 92, 117, 138, vi
Williams, C.D. 104
Williams, Denzil 37
Williams, Gerald 17
Williams, Gwynfor 11
Williams, Hilary & Luther 57
Williams, Dr John 77
Williams, J.J. 25, 144
Williams, J.P.R. 17, 27, 127
Williams, Mike 72
Williams, Ray 51-3
Williams, Richard 73
Wimbledon 50
Windhoek 146, xv
Windsor-Lewis, Geoff 75, 137
Woodward, Clive 26, 146
Wooller, Wilf 36, 110, 111
World Cup 154-7, 163, 164
World XV 27, 148
Wrexham 61

Yeandle, Andrew iii
Yorkshire 140
Young, Jack 26
Youngs, Nick xv
Ystradgynlais 58

Zambesi River 149
Zimbabwe 89, 127, 149